The BCAP Code

The UK Code of Broadcast Advertising

Edition 1

London: TSO

Published by TSO (The Stationery Office) and available from:

Online
www.tsoshop.co.uk

Mail, Telephone, Fax & E-mail
TSO
PO Box 29, Norwich, NR3 1GN
Telephone orders/General enquiries: 0870 600 5522
Fax orders: 0870 600 5533
E-mail: customer.services@tso.co.uk
Textphone 0870 240 3701

TSO@Blackwell and other Accredited Agents

Customers can also order publications from:
TSO Ireland
16 Arthur Street, Belfast BT1 4GD
Tel 028 9023 8451 Fax 028 9023 5401

First published 2010

ISBN 978 0 11 706411 9

Printed in the United Kingdom by The Stationery Office

Contents

Scheduling Rules

Appendices

Introduction

This first edition of the Code comes into force on 1 September 2010. It replaces the four previous separate BCAP Codes for broadcast advertising.

a. This Code applies to all advertisements (including teleshopping, content on self-promotional television channels, television text and interactive television advertisements) and programme sponsorship credits on radio and television services licensed by Ofcom. It is designed to inform advertisers and broadcasters of the standards expected in the content and scheduling of broadcast advertisements and to protect consumers. The basic principles of the Code are set out in Section 1: Compliance.

All Ofcom-licensed broadcasters should be familiar with the contents of this Code, which can be accessed on the ASA website, www.asa.org.uk, or the CAP website, www.cap.org.uk. They should also be familiar with relevant consumer protection legislation, most of which is listed on the CAP website at www.cap.org.uk.

b. These definitions apply to the Code:

   i. "broadcasters" means Ofcom-licensed television and radio services provided by broadcasters within UK jurisdiction regardless of whether their main audience is in the UK

   ii. "advertisement" means publicity by advertisers, including spot advertisements and broadcaster promotions with advertisers (outside programme time), that is broadcast in return for payment or other valuable consideration to a broadcaster or that seeks to sell products to viewers or listeners. The promotion of broadcasters' own-branded activities, goods and events (such as websites, T-shirts and concerts), which enhance audience involvement and are not designed to make a profit or promote commercial partnerships, are excluded

   iii. "teleshopping" means television-broadcast direct offers for the supply of goods and services, including immovable property, rights and obligations, in return for payment

   iv. The "audience" comprises all those who are likely to see or hear a given advertisement

   v. a "claim" can be implied or direct, written, spoken or visual. The name of a product can constitute a claim.

c. The Code does not apply to commercial references within a programme, for which please see the Ofcom Broadcasting Code, which is available at www.ofcom.org.uk. Ofcom requires adherence to the BCAP Code for the content of programme sponsorship credits but the ASA refers complaints about those and about product placement and undue prominence to Ofcom. "Special Category" advertisements and sponsorship credits on radio must be cleared for broadcast by the Radio Advertising Clearance Centre (RACC). Before being broadcast on radio, all advertisements that feature claims that need substantiation must be cleared locally or, if those claims are included in advertisements for a special category, by the RACC. See Section 1: Compliance.

d. Television licensees should seek BCAP's permission if they want to have any rules in the Code disapplied because the advertisement in question is on a programme service addressed exclusively to audiences outside the UK.

A television advertisement that is targeted specifically and with some frequency at an audience in the territory of a single party to the 1989 Council of Europe Convention on Transfrontier Television must, with some exceptions, comply with the television advertising rules of that party. That does not apply:

   i.   if the party is a Member State of the European Community or

   ii. if its television advertising rules discriminate between advertisements broadcast on television services within its jurisdiction and those on services outside its jurisdiction or

   iii. if the UK Government has concluded a relevant bilateral or multilateral agreement with the party concerned.

e. Advertisers, advertising agencies or independent producers should seek pre-transmission guidance on scripted advertisements from Clearcast (for TV advertisements), the RACC (for radio advertisements) or from the broadcaster whose service they intend to use to advertise. See Section 1: Compliance for information about the "special categories" of radio advertisement that require central clearance.

f. Broadcasters seeking guidance about the interpretation of Code rules should speak to BCAP staff. BCAP is willing to give advice on the interpretation of the Code but it does not offer pre-transmission clearance of advertisements. BCAP cannot accept liability for loss or damage alleged to result from reliance placed on such advice. Any advice it gives is without prejudice to the right of the ASA to investigate and act in the event of an alleged breach. BCAP can raise a potential breach of this Code with the broadcaster.

g. When the ASA feels a complaint is justified, it can take action with the broadcaster concerned. The ASA can require the broadcaster to withdraw the advertisement immediately, amend it or suspend it while investigations are carried out. The ASA Council's interpretation of the Code is final and its adjudications are published weekly on the ASA website, www.asa.org.uk. Complainants, advertisers and broadcasters may request a review of Council decisions by the Independent Reviewer of ASA Adjudications. Information about the review process is given in the Broadcast Complaint Handling Procedures document, available on the ASA website.

h. For serious or repeated breaches of the Code, Ofcom may impose sanctions, ranging from a formal warning to a request for broadcast correction or a statement of findings, a fine or the shortening, suspending or taking away of a licence to broadcast.

i. The ASA (Broadcast) Council may have regard to decisions made by the ASA (Non-broadcast) Council under the CAP Code. Similarly, the ASA (Non-broadcast) Council may have regard to decisions made by the ASA (Broadcast) Council under the BCAP Code. Factors that help to determine whether an ASA decision is likely to apply across media include, but are not limited to, the characteristics of the medium, how the advertisement is targeted, the context in which a claim is made and the extent to which the relevant BCAP Code provisions correspond to those in the CAP Code.

j. The protection of young viewers and listeners is always a priority. Section 5: Children should be considered for all advertisements that:

    i.   are targeted at children or likely to be of interest to them

    ii. features children whether as professionals or amateurs

    iii. could harmfully influence children even if not of direct interest to them.

k. Where necessary, sections of this Code begin by stating the overarching principles and background information that inform the rules subsequently given and definitions of the key terms employed.

l. Some rules that are to be found in Code sections dedicated to categories of products or services (such as alcoholic drinks or gambling) apply also to any advertisement that includes or refers to them. Those Code sections are subdivided into "rules for all advertisements" and "rules for [category of] advertisements".

m. Guidance and Help Notes referred to throughout the Code can be found at www.cap.org.uk

n. The investigation of complaints in relation to Participation TV (long form television advertising for direct-response, remote entertainment services that typically include the possibility of interacting with broadcast content) remains a matter for Ofcom. Participation TV includes, for example, long form television advertisements for adult chat, adult sex chat, psychic chat, quiz call, dating and gambling services. For the avoidance of doubt, it excludes television spot advertisements for those services. Teleshopping content promoting other goods and services is also excluded. The ASA refers complaints about Participation TV to Ofcom who will determine whether a complaint identifies a breach of the BCAP Code; the UK Code of Broadcast Advertising.

01

Compliance

Principle

The overarching principles of this Code are that advertisements should not mislead or cause serious or widespread offence or harm, especially to children or the vulnerable. Broadcasters are responsible for ensuring that the advertisements they transmit comply with both the spirit and the letter of the Code. All compliance matters (copy clearance, content, scheduling and the like) are the ultimate responsibility of each broadcaster. The ASA may decline to investigate where there is a dispute which, in its view, would be better resolved by another regulator or through the Courts.

Background

Broadcasters should use the ASA or CAP website, www.asa.org.uk and www.cap.org.uk, to inform themselves of recent ASA adjudications, the latest text of the Code and BCAP guidance on the Code.

Broadcasters must ensure that all advertisements are cleared before broadcast, are scheduled suitably and in accordance with BCAP's rules on scheduling of advertisements (Section 32: Scheduling). BCAP strongly advises broadcasters to follow relevant Clearcast or RACC scheduling warnings, although compliance with them is not necessarily a guarantee of compliance with the BCAP Code.

Broadcasters must ensure that previously approved copy is not re-run for subsequent campaigns without periodic checks to ensure that all claims are still accurate. For radio, copy originally cleared by the RACC that is over six months old will need to be re-submitted for consideration by the RACC and assigned a new clearance number. Broadcasters or their respective clearance body must independently assess evidence submitted in support of an advertisement and any advice they have commissioned. Substantiation of factual claims made by advertisers and other supporting evidence must be held by the broadcaster or the relevant clearance body.

Radio

"Special category" radio advertisements, whether broadcast locally, regionally or nationally, must be centrally cleared by the RACC. The code includes rules throughout that makes clear those categories of radio advertisement that must be centrally cleared. Broadcasters or their sales houses must hold a record of centrally cleared advertisements. For more information, go to www.racc.co.uk or telephone 020 3206 7808. The special categories are:

- Consumer credit, investment and complex financial products and services
- Gambling products and services
- Alcohol products
- Medical and health and beauty products and treatments
- Food, nutrition and food supplements
- Slimming products, treatments and establishments
- Adult shops, stripograms, escort agencies and premium-rate sexual entertainment services
- Dating and introduction services
- Commercial services offering individual personal and consumer advice
- Environmental claims

- Matters of public controversy including matters of a political or industrial nature
- Religious organisations
- Charitable causes
- Films, DVDs, video, computer and console games that have an 18+ certificate or rating.

Advertisements that do not fall into the special category list and are broadcast only by one station or in one locality must be cleared for broadcast by the relevant staff at the station concerned. Advertisers should contact the relevant station for information or guidance. To provide consistent standards for the benefit of consumers and the radio industry, national radio advertisements should be centrally cleared by the RACC. National radio advertisements are those sold and broadcast nationally across the network.

Rules

1.1   Advertisements must reflect the spirit, not merely the letter, of the Code.

1.2   Advertisements must be prepared with a sense of responsibility to the audience and to society.

1.3   Advertisements must comply with the law and broadcasters must make that a condition of acceptance.

        1.3.1   Advertisements must not state or imply that a product can legally be sold if it cannot.

02
Recognition of advertising

Background

The rules on recognition of advertising must be read in conjunction with all other parts of the Code, including Section 32: Scheduling of Advertisements. Other sections of the Code contain product-specific or audience-specific rules that are intended to protect consumers from misleading marketing communications. For example, Section 5: Children contains rules that apply, as well as the general rules, to advertisements that fall under that section.

The Ofcom Code on the Scheduling of Television Advertising and the Ofcom Broadcasting Code, for both television and radio, contain rules for sponsorship and commercial references that are relevant to this section.

Unless otherwise stated, all the rules in this section apply to programme promotions.

Definitions

"Programme" is a programme on any UK television or radio service.

"Editorial content" in this section applies to programmes on any UK television or radio service and – in rule 2.1 – to editorial content on television text services and interactive television services.

For television only: "Programme promotion" is a trailer for a programme. It is not an advertisement if it is shown on the channel on which the programme will be broadcast or on a channel related to the channel on which the programme will be broadcast.

Rules

2.1   Advertisements must be obviously distinguishable from editorial content, especially if they use a situation, performance or style reminiscent of editorial content, to prevent the audience being confused between the two. The audience should quickly recognise the message as an advertisement.

2.2   If used in an advertisement, an expression or sound effect associated with news bulletins or public service announcements (for example, "news flash") needs special care. The audience should quickly recognise the message as an advertisement.

2.3   The use of a title, logo, set or music associated with a programme that is broadcast on that medium needs special care. The audience should quickly recognise the message as an advertisement.

2.4   **Television only –** Television advertisements, except for programme promotions, must not:

    2.4.1   refer to themselves in a way that might lead viewers to believe they are watching a programme

    2.4.2   feature, visually or orally, anyone who currently and regularly presents news or current affairs on television

    2.4.3   include extracts from broadcasts of parliamentary proceedings.

2.5   **Radio only –** A person who currently and regularly reads the news on radio or television may voice radio advertisements but must not advertise products or services that are likely to be seen to compromise the impartiality of their news-reading role.

03

Misleading advertising

Background

The ASA may take the Consumer Protection from Unfair Trading Regulations 2008 into account when it adjudicates on complaints about advertisements that are alleged to be misleading. See Appendix 1 for more information about those Regulations.

The ASA will take into account the impression created by advertisements as well as specific claims. It will adjudicate on the basis of the likely effect on consumers, not the advertiser's intentions.

Other sections of the Code contain product-specific or audience-specific rules that are intended to protect consumers from misleading advertisements. For example, the Children and Medicines sections of the Code contain rules that apply, as well as the general rules, to advertisements that fall under those sections.

Rules

General

3.1   Advertisements must not materially mislead or be likely to do so.

3.2   Advertisements must not mislead consumers by omitting material information. They must not mislead by hiding material information or presenting it in an unclear, unintelligible, ambiguous or untimely manner.

Material information is information that consumers need in context to make informed decisions about whether or how to buy a product or service. Whether the omission or presentation of material information is likely to mislead consumers depends on the context, the medium and, if the medium of the advertisement is constrained by time or space, the measures that the advertiser takes to make that information available to consumers by other means.

3.3   For advertisements that quote prices for an advertised product or service, material information [for the purposes of rule 3.2] includes:

3.3.1   the main characteristics of the product or service

3.3.2   the identity (for example, a trading name) and geographical address of the marketer and any other trader on whose behalf the advertiser is acting

3.3.3   the price of the advertised product or service, including taxes, or, if the nature of the product or service is such that the price cannot be calculated in advance, the manner in which the price is calculated

3.3.4   delivery charges

3.3.5   the arrangements for payment, delivery, performance or complaint handling, if those differ from the arrangements that consumers are likely to reasonably expect

3.3.6   that consumers have the right to withdraw or cancel, if they have that right.

If the advertisement encourages consumers to buy a product or service through a distance-selling mechanism, please refer to Section 8: Distance Selling.

3.4   Obvious exaggerations ("puffery") and claims that the average consumer who sees the advertisement is unlikely to take literally are allowed provided they do not materially mislead.

3.5   Subjective claims must not mislead the audience; advertisements must not imply that expressions of opinion are objective claims.

3.6   Advertisements must not mislead by omitting the identity of the advertiser.

Rule 8.2 requires broadcasters to give enquirers the identity and geographical address of distance selling advertisers if that information is not included in the advertisement.

Advertisers should note the law requires advertisers to identify themselves in some advertisements. Advertisers should take legal advice.

3.7   Advertisements must not falsely imply that the advertiser is acting as a consumer or for purposes outside its trade, business, craft or profession. Advertisements must make clear their commercial intent, if that is not obvious from the context.

3.8   No advertisement may use images of very brief duration, or any other technique that is likely to influence consumers, without their being fully aware of what has been done.

Substantiation

3.9   Broadcasters must hold documentary evidence to prove claims that the audience is likely to regard as objective and that are capable of objective substantiation. The ASA may regard claims as misleading in the absence of adequate substantiation.

Qualification

3.10   Advertisements must state significant limitations and qualifications. Qualifications may clarify but must not contradict the claims that they qualify.

3.11   Qualifications must be presented clearly.

BCAP has published Guidance on *Superimposed Text* to help television broadcasters ensure compliance with rule 3.11.

Exaggeration

3.12   Advertisements must not mislead by exaggerating the capability or performance of a product or service.

3.13   Advertisements must not present rights given to consumers in law as a distinctive feature of the advertiser's offer.

3.14   Advertisements must not suggest that their claims are universally accepted if a significant division of informed or scientific opinion exists.

3.15   Advertisements must not mislead about the nature or extent of the risk to consumers' personal security, or that of their families, if they do not buy the advertised product or service.

Prohibited Claims

These rules apply regardless of any substantiation presented in support of the claims.

3.16   Advertisements must not claim that a product or service is able to facilitate winning in games of chance.

3.17   Advertisements must not explicitly claim that the advertiser's job or livelihood is in jeopardy if consumers do not buy the advertised product or service.

Prices

Background

Price statements in advertisements should take into account the Department for Business, Innovation and Skills (BIS) Pricing Practices Guide.

Definition

Price statements include statements about the manner in which the price will be calculated as well as definite prices.

3.18   Price statements must not mislead by omission, undue emphasis or distortion. They must relate to the product or service depicted in the advertisement.

3.19   Quoted prices must include non-optional taxes, duties, fees and charges that apply to all or most buyers. VAT-exclusive prices may be given only if all or most consumers pay no VAT or can recover VAT; advertisements that quote VAT-exclusive prices must prominently state the amount or rate of VAT payable if some consumers are likely to pay VAT.

3.20   If a tax, duty, fee or charge cannot be calculated in advance, for example, because it depends on the consumer's circumstances, the advertisement must make clear that it is excluded from the advertised price and state how it is calculated.

3.21   Advertisements that quote instalment costs must state the total price of the advertised product or service and the instalment frequency as prominently as the cost of individual instalments.

3.22   Advertisements that state prices must also state applicable delivery, freight or postal charges or, if those cannot reasonably be calculated in advance, state that such charges are payable.

3.23   If the price of one product or service depends on another, advertisements must make clear the extent of the commitment consumers must make to obtain the advertised price.

3.24   Price claims such as "up to" and "from" must not exaggerate the availability or amount of benefits likely to be obtained by consumers.

"Free" claims

Principle

Advertisements must not describe a product or service as "free", "gratis", "without charge" or similar if the consumer has to pay anything other than the unavoidable cost of responding to the promotion and collecting or paying for delivery of the item.

3.25   Advertisements must make clear the extent of the commitment consumers must make to take advantage of a "free" offer.

Advertisements must not describe items as "free" if:

3.25.1   consumers have to pay for packing, packaging, handling or administration of the "free" product or service

3.25.2   the cost of response, including the price of a product or service that consumers must buy to take advantage of the offer, has been increased, except where the increase results from factors that are unrelated to the cost of the promotion

3.25.3   the quality of the product or service that consumers must buy has been reduced

3.26   Advertisements must not describe an element of a package as "free" if that element is included in the package price, unless consumers are likely to regard it as an additional benefit because it has recently been added to the package without increasing its price.

3.27   Advertisements must not use the term "free trial" to describe a "satisfaction or your money back" offer or an offer for which a non-refundable purchase is required.

         BCAP and CAP have published joint guidance on the use of "free".

Availability

3.28   Broadcasters must be satisfied that advertisers have made a reasonable estimate of demand.

3.29   Advertisements that quote prices for featured products must state any reasonable grounds the advertisers have for believing that they might not be able to supply the advertised (or an equivalent) product at the advertised price, within a reasonable period and in reasonable quantities. In particular:

         3.29.1   if estimated demand exceeds supply, advertisements must make clear that stock is limited

         3.29.2   if the advertiser does not intend to fulfil orders, because the purpose of the advertisement is to assess potential demand, the advertisement must make that clear

         3.29.3   advertisements must not mislead consumers by omitting restrictions on the availability of products; for example, geographical restrictions or age limits.

3.30   Broadcasters must be satisfied that advertisers who advertise products at specific prices will not use the technique of switch selling, in which their sales staff refuse to show the advertised product, refuse to take orders for it or to deliver it within a reasonable time or demonstrate a defective sample of it to promote a different product.

3.31   Advertisements must not falsely claim that the advertiser is about to stop trading or move premises. They must not falsely state that a product or service, or the terms on which it is offered, will be available only for a very limited time to deprive consumers of the time or opportunity to make an informed choice.

3.32   Advertisements must not mislead consumers about market conditions or the possibility of finding the product or service elsewhere to induce consumers to buy the product or service at conditions less favourable than normal market conditions.

Comparisons

Principle

The ASA will consider unqualified superlative claims as comparative claims against all competing products or services.

Superiority claims must be supported by evidence unless they are obvious puffery (that is, claims that consumers are unlikely to take literally). Objective superiority claims must make clear the aspect of the product or service or the advertiser's performance that is claimed to be superior.

Comparisons with Identifiable Competitors

3.33   Advertisements that include a comparison with an identifiable competitor must not mislead, or be likely to mislead, consumers about either the advertised product or service or the competing product or service.

3.34   Advertisements must compare products or services meeting the same need or intended for the same purpose.

3.35   Advertisements must objectively compare one or more material, relevant, verifiable and representative feature of those products or services.

3.36   Advertisements must not create confusion between the advertiser and its competitors or between the advertiser's product or service, trade mark, trade name or other distinguishing mark and that of a competitor.

3.37   Certain EU agricultural products and foods are, because of their unique geographical area and method of production, given special protection by being registered as having a "designation of origin". Products that are registered as having a "designation of origin" should be compared only with other products with the same designation.

Other Comparisons

3.38   Advertisements that include comparisons with unidentifiable competitors must not mislead, or be likely to mislead, consumers. The elements of the comparison must not be selected to give the advertiser an unrepresentative advantage.

Price Comparisons

3.39   Advertisements that include a price comparison must state the basis of the comparison. Comparisons with competitors' prices must be with the prices for identical or substantially equivalent products or services and must explain significant differences between the products or services. If the competitor offers more than one similar product or service, the advertisement must compare the advertiser's price with the price for the competitor's product or service that is most similar to the advertised product or service.

3.40   Price comparisons must not mislead by falsely claiming a price advantage. Comparisons with recommended retail prices (RRPs) are likely to mislead if the RRP differs significantly from the price at which the product or service is generally sold.

Imitation and Denigration

3.41   Advertisements must not mislead consumers about who manufactures the product.

3.42   Advertisements must not discredit or denigrate another product, advertiser or advertisement or a trade mark, trade name or other distinguishing mark.

3.43   Advertisements must not take unfair advantage of the reputation of a competitor's trade mark, trade name or other distinguishing mark or of the designation of origin of a competitor product or service.

3.44   Advertisements must not present a product as an imitation or replica of a product or service with a protected trade mark or trade name.

Endorsements and Testimonials

Background

Advertisements that include endorsements or testimonials might also be subject to Section 6: Privacy.

3.45   Testimonials or endorsements used in advertising must be genuine, unless they are obviously fictitious, and be supported by documentary evidence. Testimonials and endorsements must relate to the advertised product or service. Claims that are likely to be interpreted as factual and appear in advertisements must not mislead or be likely to mislead.

3.46   Advertisements must not feature testimonials without permission.

3.47   Advertisements must not display a trust mark, quality mark or equivalent without the necessary authorisation. Advertisements must not claim that the advertiser (or any other entity referred to in the advertisement), the advertisement or the advertised product or service has been approved, endorsed or authorised by any person or body if it has not or without complying with the terms of the approval, endorsement or authorisation.

3.48   Advertisements must not falsely claim that the advertiser, or other entity referred to in the advertisement, is a signatory to a code of conduct. Advertisements must not falsely claim that a code of conduct has an endorsement from a public or other body.

Guarantees and After-sales Service

3.49 Advertisements must not use the word "guarantee" in a way that could cause confusion about a consumer's rights.

3.50 Advertisements must make clear each significant limitation to an advertised guarantee (of the type that has implications for a consumer's rights). Broadcasters must be satisfied that the advertiser will supply the full terms of the guarantee before the consumer is committed to taking it up.

3.51 Broadcasters must be satisfied that advertiser will promptly refund consumers who make valid claims under an advertised money-back guarantee.

3.52 Advertisements must not falsely claim or imply that after-sales service is available in an EEA member state in which the advertised product or service is not sold.

3.53 If an advertisement in a language other than an official language of the EEA State where the trader is located offers after-sales service but the after-sales service is not available in the language of the advertisement, broadcasters must be satisfied that the advertiser will explain that to consumers before a contract is concluded.

04

Harm and offence

Principle

Advertisements must not be harmful or offensive. Advertisements must take account of generally accepted standards to minimise the risk of causing harm or serious or widespread offence. The context in which an advertisement is likely to be broadcast must be taken into account to avoid unsuitable scheduling (see Section 32: Scheduling).

Rules

4.1   Advertisements must contain nothing that could cause physical, mental, moral or social harm to persons under the age of 18.

4.2   Advertisements must not cause serious or widespread offence against generally accepted moral, social or cultural standards.

4.3   Advertisements must not exploit the special trust that persons under the age of 18 place in parents, guardians, teachers or other persons.

4.4   Advertisements must not include material that is likely to condone or encourage behaviour that prejudices health or safety.

4.5   **Radio only** – Advertisements must not include sounds that are likely to create a safety hazard, for example, to those listening to the radio while driving.

4.6   **Television only** – Advertisements must not include visual effects or techniques that are likely to affect adversely members of the audience with photosensitive epilepsy (see Ofcom's *Guidance Note for Licensees on Flashing Images and Regular Patterns in Television*).

4.7   **Television only** – Advertisements must not be excessively noisy or strident. The maximum subjective loudness of advertisements must be consistent and in line with the maximum loudness of programmes and junction material.

Broadcasters must endeavour to minimise the annoyance that perceived imbalances could cause, with the aim that the audience need not adjust the volume of their television sets during programme breaks. For editorial reasons, however, commercial breaks sometimes occur during especially quiet parts of a programme, with the result that advertisements at normally acceptable levels seem loud in comparison.

Measurement and balancing of subjective loudness levels should preferably be carried out using a loudness-level meter, ideally conforming to ITU recommendations[1]. If a peak-reading meter[2] is used instead, the maximum level of the advertisements must be at least 6dB less than the maximum level of the programmes[3] to take account of the limited dynamic range exhibited by most advertisements.

4.8   Advertisements must not condone or encourage harmful discriminatory behaviour or treatment. Advertisements must not prejudice respect for human dignity.

4.9   Advertisements must not condone or encourage violence, crime, disorder or anti-social behaviour.

4.10   Advertisements must not distress the audience without justifiable reason. Advertisements must not exploit the audience's fears or superstitions.

4.11   **Television only –** Animals must not be harmed or distressed as a result of the production of an advertisement.

4.12   Advertisements must not condone or encourage behaviour grossly prejudicial to the protection of the environment.

---

1   The relevant ITU recommendations are ITU-R BS1770 Algorithms to measure audio programme loudness and true-peak audio level and ITU-R BS1771 Requirements for loudness and true-peak indicating meters.

2   Peak-reading meters should be a PPM Type IIa as specified in BS6840: Part 10, Programme Level Meters.

3   Normal convention for analogue audio is that the peak sound level of programmes is set to be no higher than +8dBm, which corresponds to 6 on a peak-reading meter. The peak sound level of advertisements should therefore be limited to +2dBm or 4.5 on a peak-reading meter. Note: +8dBm corresponds to a digital audio level of -10dB relative to digital clipping level. ITU-R BS.645 and EBU recommendation R68-2000 describe how analogue audio levels should be translated into digital levels.

05
Children

Principle

Children must be protected from advertisements that could cause physical, mental or moral harm.

Background

The context in which an advertisement is likely to be broadcast and the likely age of the audience must be taken into account to avoid unsuitable scheduling. Advertisements that are suitable for older children and young persons but could distress younger children must be sensitively scheduled or placed. This section should therefore be read in conjunction with Section 32: Scheduling. Care must be taken when scheduling advertisements that could frighten or distress children or could otherwise be unsuitable for them: those advertisements should not be scheduled or placed in or around children's programmes or in or around programmes likely to be seen by significant numbers of children. Care must also be taken when featuring children in advertisements.

Definitions

A child is someone under 16.

"Children's products and services" are products or services of more or less exclusive interest to children.

"Products and services of interest to children" are products or services that are likely to appeal to children but are not of exclusive interest to them.

Rules

5.1   Advertisements that are suitable for older children but could distress younger children must be sensitively scheduled (see Section 32: Scheduling).

5.2   Advertisements must not condone, encourage or unreasonably feature behaviour that could be dangerous for children to emulate. Advertisements must not implicitly or explicitly discredit established safety guidelines. Advertisements must not condone, encourage or feature children going off alone or with strangers.

This rule is not intended to prevent advertisements that inform children about dangers or risks associated with potentially harmful behaviour.

5.3   Advertisements must not condone or encourage practices that are detrimental to children's health.

5.4   Advertisements must not condone or encourage bullying.

5.5   Advertisements must not portray or represent children in a sexual way.

5.6   Advertisements must not imply that children are likely to be ridiculed, inferior to others, less popular, disloyal or have let someone down if they or their family do not use a product or service.

5.7   Advertisements must not take advantage of children's inexperience, credulity or sense of loyalty. Advertisements for products or services of interest to children must not be likely to mislead; for example, by exaggerating the features of a product or service in a way that could lead to children having unrealistic expectations of that product or service.

5.8   Child actors may feature in advertisements but care must be taken to ensure that those advertisements neither mislead nor exploit children's inexperience, credulity or sense of loyalty.

5.9   Advertisements must neither directly exhort children to buy a product or service nor encourage them to ask their parents, guardians or other persons to buy or enquire about a product or service for them.

5.10   Advertisements that promote a product or service and invite consumers to buy that product or service via a direct response mechanism must not be targeted directly at children. For a definition of "direct response mechanism", see Section 8: Distance Selling.

5.11   If it includes a price, an advertisement for a children's product or service must not use qualifiers such as "only" or "just" to make the price seem less expensive.

5.12   **Television only –** Advertisements for a toy, game or comparable children's product must include a statement of its price or, if it is not possible to include a precise price, an approximate price, if that product costs £30 or more.

5.13   Advertisements for promotions targeted directly at children:

5.13.1   must include all significant qualifying conditions

5.13.2   must make clear if adult permission is required for children to enter.

Advertisements for competitions targeted directly at children are acceptable only if the skill required is relevant to the age of likely participants and if the values of the prizes and the chances of winning are not exaggerated.

5.14   Promotions that require a purchase to participate and include a direct exhortation to make a purchase must not be targeted directly at children.

Advertisements for promotions directly targeted at children should comply with Section 28: Competitions.

06
Privacy

Principle

Living individuals should be protected from unwarranted infringements of privacy. Broadcasters should respect an individual's right to his or her private and family life, home and correspondence. Advertisements featuring an individual should not imply that that individual endorses a product if he or she does not (see Section 3: Misleading Advertising).

Rules

6.1   **Television only –** With limited exceptions, living persons must not be featured, caricatured or referred to in advertisements without their permission.

Exceptions are made only for brief and incidental appearances, such as crowd scenes, and advertisements that refer to a person featured in publications, programmes, films and the like, providing that the reference to or portrayal of that person is neither offensive nor defamatory.

6.2   **Radio only –** Broadcasters must ensure that, if an advertiser has not sought his or her prior permission, a person featured in an advertisement must not be featured in an offensive, adverse or defamatory way.

Advertisements that feature, allude or refer to a living person must not interfere with that person's private or family life: legal advice is strongly advisable and is required in cases of doubt. Advertisements that feature, caricature or refer to a living person will be cleared on the basis that it is recommended that that person's permission is sought. Even if an advertisement contains nothing that is inconsistent with the position or views of the person featured, broadcasters and advertisers should be aware that those who do not want to be associated with the advertised product might have a legal claim.

Impersonations, soundalikes, parodies or similar take-offs of celebrities are permissible only if those devices are instantly recognisable and if it could be reasonably expected that the person concerned has no reason to object. Nevertheless, advertisers are urged to obtain advance permission or seek legal advice before clearance. Copyright permission should be sought for references to, or portrayals of, well-known characters or their names or personae.

07

Political and controversial matters

Background

The Communications Act 2003 prohibits political advertising. The term "political" is used in the Code in a wider sense than "party political". The prohibition includes, for example, campaigning for the purposes of influencing legislation or executive action by local or national (including foreign) governments. The definitions of "political" for the purposes of an advertiser's status and for the content of advertisements are set out in section 321 of the Communications Act 2003 ("the Act"). The relevant parts of that section are reproduced below in Rule 7.2.

Responsibility for the application of the rules that prohibit "political" advertising and whether an advertiser and/or the content of an advertisement is caught by the prohibition has not been contracted out to BCAP or the ASA. This responsibility remains with Ofcom. The ASA therefore refers all such matters to Ofcom.

Rules

7.1   **Radio Central Copy Clearance** – Radio broadcasters must seek central clearance for advertisements that might fall under this section on the grounds of either the advertiser's objectives or the content of the advertisement.

7.2   Advertising that contravenes the prohibition on political advertising set out below must not be included in television or radio services;

    7.2.1   An advertisement contravenes the prohibition on political advertising if it is:

        (a) an advertisement which is inserted by or on behalf of a body whose objects are wholly or mainly of a political nature;

        (b) an advertisement which is directed towards a political end; or

        (c) an advertisement which has a connection with an industrial dispute.

7.2.2   For the purposes of this section objects of a political nature and political ends include each of the following:

        (a) influencing the outcome of elections or referendums, whether in the United Kingdom or elsewhere;

        (b) bringing about changes of the law in the whole or a part of the United Kingdom or elsewhere, or otherwise influencing the legislative process in any country or territory;

        (c) influencing the policies or decisions of local, regional or national governments, whether in the United Kingdom or elsewhere;

        (d) influencing the policies or decisions of persons on whom public functions are conferred by or under the law of the United Kingdom or of a country or territory outside the United Kingdom;

(e) influencing the policies or decisions of persons on whom functions are conferred by or under international agreements;

(f) influencing public opinion on a matter which, in the United Kingdom, is a matter of public controversy;

(g) promoting the interests of a party or other group of persons organised, in the United Kingdom or elsewhere, for political ends.

7.2.3   Provision included by virtue of this section in standards set under section 319 [of the Act] is not to apply to, or to be construed as prohibiting the inclusion in a programme service of:

(a) an advertisement of a public service nature inserted by, or on behalf of, a government department; or

(b) a party political or referendum campaign broadcast the inclusion of which is required by a condition imposed under section 333 [of the Act] or by paragraph 18 of Schedule 12 to the Act.

08

Distance selling

Background

Most distance selling contracts are subject to the Consumer Protection (Distance Selling) Regulations 2000 (as amended). These rules complement those Regulations and do not replace them. Broadcasters that operate as teleshopping channels should seek legal advice to ensure they comply with the Regulations.

Definitions

The rules in this section apply to advertisements that promote specific products or services and invite consumers to buy those products or services, without meeting the supplier face-to-face, by means of direct response mechanisms, except advertisements for

> a. the sale of land
>
> b. the construction of a building, if that includes the sale of land
>
> c. financial services, which are covered by Section 14: Financial Products, Services and Investments.

Teleshopping broadcasters are the advertisers of all products and services that are promoted in their services.

These rules should be read in conjunction with other rules in this Code, especially the rules of availability in Section 3: Misleading Advertising and, for advertisements that quote prices, rule 3.3.

Rules

8.1 **Radio Central Copy Clearance –** Radio advertisements subject to this section must be centrally cleared.

8.2 Broadcasters must be able to give consumers the advertiser's name and geographical address for complaints if that information is not included in the advertisement.

8.3 Broadcasters must be satisfied that the advertisers:

> **8.3.1** have made adequate arrangements to protect consumers' money
>
> **8.3.2** can take enquiries during normal business hours
>
> **8.3.3** make samples of the advertised products available for public inspection, pre-clearance and investigation of complaints about claims made in advertisements for the product
>
> **8.3.4** tell consumers if they intend to supply substitute products or services if the advertised product or service becomes unavailable
>
> **8.3.5** fulfil orders within 30 days unless

a. the nature of the product or service makes it reasonable to specify a longer period in the advertisement; for example, advertisements for made-to-measure products, plants that are out of season, or products or services that are supplied on an instalment basis may reasonably specify a longer period or

b. a longer performance period has been agreed with the consumer

8.3.6 give refunds in accordance with rule 8.4

8.3.7 will not seek payment for products or services that are supplied without the recipient's authority

8.3.8 inform consumers about their cancellation rights.

8.4 Advertisers must give refunds within 30 days if the consumer cancels, for any reason, within seven days of receiving goods or seven clear days from the conclusion of a contract for services, unless

a. performance of the service has already begun, with the consumer's agreement

b. the price of the product or service is dependent on fluctuations in the financial market beyond the control of the advertiser

c. the product is perishable, personalised or made-to-measure

d. the product is an audio or video recording or computer software unsealed by the consumer

e. the product is a newspaper, periodical or magazine

f. the service is a betting, gaming or lottery service.

8.5 Advertisers must give a refund if the consumer can show reasonable cause for dissatisfaction with the product or service or delay in delivery.

Except for substitute goods supplied in place of the goods that the consumer ordered, and faulty goods, advertisers may require consumers to pay the direct cost of returning goods ordered through a distance selling mechanism if the consumers were informed before the contract was concluded that they would be liable for the cost of returning unwanted goods.

09

Environmental claims

Background

Advertisements should take account of Government guidance including the Green Claims Code published by DEFRA and BIS.

Rules

9.1 **Radio Central Copy Clearance –** Radio broadcasters must ensure advertisements subject to this section are centrally cleared.

9.2 The basis of environmental claims must be clear. Unqualified claims could mislead if they omit significant information.

9.3 The meaning of all terms used in advertisements must be clear to consumers.

9.4 Absolute claims must be supported by a high level of substantiation. Comparative claims such as "greener" or "friendlier" can be justified, for example, if the advertised product or service provides a total environmental benefit over that of the advertiser's previous product or service or competitor products or services and the basis of the comparison is clear.

9.5 Environmental claims must be based on the full life cycle of the advertised product or service, unless the advertisement states otherwise, and must make clear the limits of the life cycle. If a general claim cannot be justified, a more limited claim about specific aspects of a product or service might be justifiable. Claims that are based on only part of an advertised product or service's life cycle must not mislead consumers about the product or service's total environmental impact.

9.6 Advertisements must not suggest that their claims are universally accepted if a significant division of informed or scientific opinion exists.

9.7 If a product or service has never had a demonstrably adverse effect on the environment, advertisements must not imply that the formulation has changed to improve the product or service in the way claimed. Advertisements may, however, claim that a product or service has always been designed in a way that omits an ingredient or process known to harm the environment.

9.8 Advertisements must not mislead consumers about the environmental benefit that a product or service offers; for example, by highlighting the absence of an environmentally damaging ingredient if that ingredient is not usually found in competing products or services by highlighting an environmental benefit that results from a legal obligation if competing products are subject to the same requirements.

10

Prohibited categories

Principle

Broadcast advertisements for some products or services are not permitted either because those products may not legally be advertised or because of a clear potential for harm or serious or widespread offence to the audience or to society.

Background

There are other unacceptable and restricted categories of advertising not listed in this Section, which can be found in these sections: Political and Controversial Matters (Section 7); Children (Section 5); Medicines, Medical Devices, Treatments and Health (Section 11); Financial Products, Services and Investments (Section 14); Faith, Religion and Equivalent Systems of Belief (Section 15); Homeworking Schemes (Section 24); Instructional Courses (Section 25) and Pornography (Section 30).

Rules

10.1   Advertisements for products or services coming within the recognised character of or specifically concerned with these are not acceptable:

10.1.1   breath-testing devices and products that are intended to mask the effects of alcohol

10.1.2   betting systems and products that are intended to facilitate winning games of chance

10.1.3   all tobacco products. Also non-tobacco products or services that share a name, emblem or other feature with a tobacco product (as provided for by rule 10.4), rolling papers and filters

10.1.4   guns (including replica guns), gun clubs and offensive weapons. "Offensive weapons" are items made or adapted to cause injury. References to clay pigeon shoots are permitted only as part of a wider range of outdoor pursuits

10.1.5   prostitution and sexual massage services

10.1.6   obscene material. "Obscene material" is material that offends against the Obscene Publications Act 1959 (as amended)

10.1.7   products for the treatment of alcohol and illegal-substance dependence

10.1.8   pyramid promotional schemes. "Pyramid promotional schemes" are those in which consumers pay or give other consideration for the opportunity to receive compensation that is derived primarily from the introduction of other consumers into the scheme, not the sale or consumption of products

10.1.9   the acquisition or disposal of units in collective investment schemes not authorised or recognised by the FSA, without the prior approval of BCAP.

10.1.10   **Television only –** Escort agencies

10.2   No advertisement may indirectly promote an unacceptable product or service. For example, advertisements must not refer the audience to a website or a publication if a significant part of that website or publication promotes a prohibited product or service.

Tobacco

10.3   Advertisements must not promote smoking or the use of tobacco products.

10.4   If it shares a name, emblem or other feature with a tobacco product, a non-tobacco product or service may be advertised only if the advertisement is obviously directly targeted at an adult audience, makes or implies no reference to smoking or to a tobacco product, does not promote tobacco or smoking and does not include a design, colour, imagery, logo style or the like that might be associated in the audience's mind with a tobacco product.

10.5   Advertisements that might be of particular interest to children or teenagers must not refer to tobacco or smoking, unless that reference obviously forms part of an anti-smoking or anti-drugs message.

11

Medicines, medical devices, treatments and health

Background

The rules in this section are designed to ensure that advertisements that include health claims (please see Section 13 for health claims made on foods) and advertisements for medicines, medical devices and treatments receive the necessary high level of scrutiny. Health claims may, for example, relate to the therapeutic or prophylactic effects of products, including toiletries and cosmetics.

The rules apply to advertisements and not the products or services, which are regulated by health regulators such as the Medicines and Healthcare products Regulatory Agency (MHRA), the European Medicines Agency (EMEA), the Care Quality Commission and the Department of Health. Advertisements for those products or services must comply with the rules and professional codes of conduct of relevant professional bodies.

Medical advisory panels

For television advertisements, Clearcast retains a panel of consultants to advise it on health and medical aspects of products or services before they are advertised. For information, see "Contact us" at www.clearcast.co.uk.

For radio advertisements, the RACC retains a panel of consultants to advise it on health and medical aspects of advertising. For information, see "Services" at www.racc.co.uk.

The ASA or BCAP may seek a medical opinion if there is a significant challenge to an advertisement that has been accepted by a broadcaster on the advice of a member of the panels.

Law

Advertisements for products subject to licensing under the Medicines Act 1968 must comply with the requirements of the Act. That includes regulations made under the Act and any conditions contained in the marketing authorisation, certificate, licence or traditional herbal registration for the advertised product.

Title VIII of European Directive 2001/83/EC as amended by Directive 2004/27/EC concerns "The Advertising of Medicinal Products for Human Use" and has been implemented in the UK by The Medicines (Advertising) Regulations 1994 and The Medicines (Monitoring of Advertising) Regulations 1994 (both as amended). ASA (Broadcast) is obliged to consider complaints about breaches of Regulation 9 of the Advertising Regulations, which has been incorporated in these rules.

With the introduction of new or changed products, the diverse licensing requirements of the Medicines Act 1968 and changes in medical opinion, this Code cannot provide a complete guide to all requirements for health claims or the advertising of products or classes of medicines and treatments.

The rules governing the advertising of medicines, treatments, medical devices and health claims are set out below; they apply also to advertisements for veterinary products and services. Directive 2001/82/EC on the Community code relating to veterinary medicinal products (as amended by Directive 2004/28/EC), which has been implemented in the UK via The Veterinary Medicines Regulations, contains provisions relating to the advertising of such products. The Veterinary Medicines Regulations are revoked and remade annually.

For more information on medicinal products and treatments, go to: www.mhra.gov.uk.

The European legislation governing medical devices is made up of Directive 90/385/EEC relating to active implantable medical devices, Directive 93/42/EEC on medical devices (as amended by Directive 2000/70/EC) and Directive 98/79/EC on in-vitro diagnostic medical devices. The MHRA is the body responsible for ensuring medical devices work and are safe. Generally, all devices covered by the scope of the relevant Directive should carry a CE mark, which is a public representation of the manufacturer's claim that its device satisfies the relevant Essential Requirements of the Directives, is fit for its intended purpose and, if required, has been independently assessed by a Notified Body. For more information, go to: www.mhra.gov.uk.

Definition

For the purposes of this section, "licence" includes certificate, authorisation or registration.

Rules

11.1 **Radio Central Copy Clearance –** Radio broadcasters must ensure advertisements subject to this section are centrally cleared.

11.2 If they are necessary for the assessment of claims, broadcasters must, before the advertisement is broadcast, obtain generally accepted scientific evidence and independent expert advice.

11.3 Advertisements must not discourage essential treatment for conditions for which medical supervision should be sought. For example, they must not offer specific advice on, diagnosis of or treatment for such conditions unless that advice, diagnosis or treatment is conducted under the supervision of a suitably qualified health professional (see rule 11.9). That does not prevent advertising for spectacles, contact lenses or hearing aids.

11.4   Medicinal or medical claims and indications may be made for a medicinal product that is licensed by the MHRA or EMEA, or for a CE-marked medical device. A medicinal claim is a claim that a product or its constituent(s) can be used with a view to making a medical diagnosis or can treat or prevent disease, including an injury, ailment or adverse condition, whether of body or mind, in human beings.

Secondary medicinal claims made for cosmetic products as defined in the appropriate European legislation must be backed by evidence. These are limited to any preventative action of the product and may not include claims to treat disease.

11.5   These are not acceptable in advertisements for medicinal products:

11.5.1   Presentations, by doctors, dentists, veterinary surgeons, pharmaceutical chemists, nurses, midwives and the like that imply professional advice or recommendation

11.5.2   statements that imply professional advice or recommendation by people who are presented, whether directly or by implication, as being qualified to give that advice or recommendation

11.5.3   references to approval of, or preference for, any relevant product or their use by the professions covered by rule 11.5.1.

11.6   Advertisements other than those for medicinal products may feature or refer to health professionals covered by rule 11.5.1, if those professionals are suitably qualified in the relevant subject.

11.7   Unless it is obvious from the context, advertisements that include a health professional must make clear if he or she has a direct financial interest, or equivalent reciprocal interest, in the sale of the advertised product or service.

11.8   Testimonials or endorsements by health professionals must be genuine and supported by documentary evidence. Fictitious testimonials must not be presented as genuine. Any statement in a testimonial that is likely to be interpreted as a factual claim must be substantiated.

11.9   **Services including Clinics, Establishments and the like Offering Advice on, or Treatment in, Medical, Personal or other Health Matters –** Advertisements are acceptable only if the advertiser can provide suitable credentials, for example, evidence of: relevant professional expertise or qualifications; systems for regular review of their skills and competencies and suitable professional indemnity insurance covering all services provided; accreditation by a professional or regulatory body that has systems for dealing with complaints and taking disciplinary action and has registration based on minimum standards for training and qualifications.

11.10   Advertisements for hypnosis-based procedures (including techniques commonly referred to as hypnotherapy), psychiatry, psychology, psychoanalysis or psychotherapy are acceptable subject to rule 11.9. Broadcasters must take particular care over advertisements for publications employing those techniques.

11.11

> **11.11.1**   **Radio only** – Advertisements for family planning centres are not acceptable unless the family planning centre has been approved by a Local Health Authority, the Central Office of Information or other appropriate NHS body.
>
> **11.11.2**   **Radio Central Copy Clearance** – Radio broadcasters must ensure advertisements for family planning centres are centrally cleared.
>
> **11.11.3**   **Television only** – Advertisements for commercial post-conception advice services offering individual advice on personal problems are not acceptable.
>
> Given that abortions are lawful only in exceptional circumstances, and are subject to particularly stringent requirements in Northern Ireland, broadcasters may wish to seek legal advice before advertising.
>
> See also rule 11.9, Section 15: Faith, Religion and Equivalent Systems of Belief and Section 16: Charities.

11.12   **Television only** – Teleshopping for these products or services is not acceptable:

> **11.12.1**   medicinal products that are for human use and that are subject to a marketing authorisation within the meaning of Directive 2001/83/EC (as amended by Directive 2004/27/EC) and are on the General Sale List (GSL) as a pharmacy medicine (P) or as a prescription-only medicine (POM)
>
> **11.12.2**   veterinary medicinal products that are subject to a marketing authorisation within the meaning of Directive 2001/82/EC (as amended by Directive 2004/28/EC) and are available as an authorised veterinary medicine on the General Sales List (AVMGSL) as a non-food animal medicine from a veterinarian, pharmacist or suitably qualified person or as a prescription-only medicine from a veterinarian (POM-V) or from a veterinarian, pharmacist or suitably qualified person (POM-VPS)
>
> **11.12.3**   medical treatments for humans or animals.

11.13   Broadcasters may accept advertisements for services offering remote personalised advice on medical or health matters only if all staff providing that advice are suitably qualified and subject to regulation by a statutory or recognised medical or health professional body and the advice given is in accordance with its relevant professional codes of conduct (see rule 11.9).

    11.13.1   Advertisements must not contain offers to prescribe or treat remotely (including by phone, post, e-mail or fax). That does not preclude advertisements containing offers to distribute general information on health-related matters, such as leaflets or information packs.

11.14   No advertisement may encourage indiscriminate, unnecessary or excessive use of products or services covered by this section.

11.15   Unless allowed by a product licence, words, phrases or illustrations that claim or imply the cure of an ailment, illness, disease or addiction, as distinct from the relief of its symptoms, are unacceptable.

11.16   Unless authorised by the relevant product licence, the word "tonic" is not acceptable in advertisements that make health claims. Claims must not suggest that a product has tonic properties. That does not prevent the use of the word "tonic" in the description "Indian tonic water" or "quinine tonic water".

11.17   Jingles may be used. Those that incorporate a medical or health claim must be substantiated.

11.18   Advertisements for smoking deterrents:

    11.18.1   must make clear that the indispensable factor in giving up smoking is willpower

    11.18.2   must not claim that smoking is safer while the habit is being reduced.

Medicines

11.19   Medicines must have a licence from the MHRA before they are advertised. Advertisements for medicinal products must conform with the licence. Advertisements must not suggest that a product is "special" or "different" because it has been granted a licence from the MHRA. For the avoidance of doubt, by conforming with the product's indicated use, an advertisement would not breach rule 11.3.

11.20   Advertisements for medicinal products which include a product claim (including legible on-pack product claims within a pack shot) must include this information:

    11.20.1   the name of the product

    11.20.2   the name of the active ingredient, if it contains only one

    11.20.3   relevant wording such as "always read the label" or "always read the leaflet"

11.20.4   the indication (what the product is for).

Advertisements for traditional herbal medicinal products and homeopathic medicinal products must include mandatory information, which can be found in the *MHRA Blue Guide* at www.mhra.gov.uk.

11.21   Advertisements for these are not acceptable:

11.21.1   medicinal products or medical treatments available only on prescription

11.21.2   Products for the treatment of alcohol or substance misuse or dependence. An exception is made for smoking deterrents (see rule 11.18).

11.22   No advertisement may suggest that a medicinal product is a foodstuff, cosmetic or other consumer product.

11.23   No advertisement for a medicinal product may claim its effects are guaranteed. That does not prevent the offering of refunds, if the advertisement does not suggest that efficacy is guaranteed.

11.24   No advertisement for a medicinal product or treatment may be directed at children. See also Section 5: Children and Section 32: Scheduling.

11.25   Advertisements must not, without good reason, make the audience anxious that they are or might be suffering from disease or ill-health or might do so if they do not respond to the advertisement.

11.25.1   Advertisements must not falsely suggest that a product is necessary for the maintenance of physical or mental health or that health could be enhanced by taking the product or affected by not taking it.

11.26   Advertisements must not, in improper, alarming or misleading ways, use images of changes in the human body caused by disease, injury or a medicinal product.

11.27   No advertisement for a medicinal product or treatment may include a recommendation by a person well-known in public life, sport, entertainment or similar or be presented by such a person. That includes persons corporate as well as singular and would prohibit, for example, recommendations by medical charities, patient groups and health or sport organisations.

11.28   No advertisement for a medicinal product may refer in improper, alarming or misleading terms to claims of recovery.

11.29   Advertisements for medicinal products must not contain material that could, for example, by description or detailed representation of a case history, lead to a wrong self-diagnosis.

11.30   Although it may refer to the likely absence of a specific side effect, for example, "unlikely to cause drowsiness", no advertisement for a medicinal product may suggest that a product has no side effects.

11.31   No advertisement for a medicinal product or treatment may suggest that the effects are better than, or equivalent to, those of another identifiable medicinal product or treatment.

11.32   No advertisement for a medicinal product may suggest that the safety or efficacy of the product is due to it being "natural".

11.33   Only homeopathic medicinal products that are registered in the UK may be advertised. Mandatory information for homeopathic advertisements can be found in the *MHRA Blue Guide* at www.mhra.gov.uk.

11.34   A tension headache is a recognised medical condition; analgesics may be advertised for the relief of pain associated with that condition but no advertisement for a simple or compound analgesic may claim the direct relief of tension or refer to depression.

12

Weight control and slimming

Background

The rules in this section are designed to ensure that advertisements for weight control and slimming products and services receive the necessary high level of scrutiny.

Definitions

This section applies to advertisements for weight-control and slimming foodstuffs, aids (including exercise products that make weight-loss or slimming claims), clinics and other establishments, diets, medicines, treatments and the like. If applicable, they must comply with Section 11: Medicines, Medical Devices, Treatments and Health or Section 13: Food, Food Supplements and Associated Health or Nutrition Claims.

Rules

12.1   **Radio Central Copy Clearance –** Radio broadcasters must ensure advertisements subject to this Section are centrally cleared.

12.2   If they are necessary for the assessment of claims, broadcasters must, before the advertisement is broadcast, obtain generally accepted scientific evidence and independent expert advice.

12.3   Advertisements for services offering remote personalised advice on health matters related to weight control or slimming are acceptable only if all staff providing that advice are suitably qualified and subject to regulation by a statutory or recognised medical or health professional body and the advice given is in accordance with its relevant professional code of conduct (see rule 11.9). That does not prevent advertisements that offer general information on health matters related to slimming or weight control.

12.4   Advertisements must not encourage indiscriminate or excessive use of a weight-control or slimming product or service.

12.5   Advertisements for slimming or weight control products or services must not be addressed to people under 18, use creative treatments likely to be of particular appeal to them, or feature any person whose example people under 18 are likely to follow or who has a particular appeal to them. This rule does not apply to advertisements for calorie-reduced or energy-reduced foods and drinks, provided the product is not presented as part of a slimming regime and the advertisement does not use the theme of slimming or weight control.

12.6   Broadcasters must obtain suitably qualified independent medical advice or other suitably qualified health specialist advice on the safety and efficacy of weight control and slimming products or services before broadcast. In particular, the advice must satisfy broadcasters that:

  12.6.1   the slimming product or service is likely to be effective and will not lead to harm

  12.6.2   clinics and other establishments offering medically supervised treatments are run in accordance with the National Minimum Standards Regulations issued by the Department of Health or, if they operate abroad, broadly equivalent requirements.

12.7   Promises or predictions of specific weight loss are not acceptable for any slimming product.

12.8   Health claims in food product advertisements that refer to a rate or amount of weight loss are not permitted.

12.9   Claims that refer to specific amounts of weight that have been lost by an individual must state the period over which that loss was achieved and should not be based on unrepresentative experiences of the slimming or weight-control product or service (see rule 12.8). The amount of weight lost and the period over which it was lost must be compatible with generally accepted good medical and dietary practice. For those who are normally overweight, a rate of weight loss greater than 2lbs (just under 1kg) a week is unlikely to be compatible with good medical and nutritional practice. For those who are obese, a rate of weight loss greater than 2lbs a week in the early stages of dieting could be compatible with good medical and nutritional practice.

12.10   Low-calorie foods and drinks, if advertised as, or as part of, a slimming regime or if advertised using a slimming or weight-control theme, must make clear in the advertisement that the product merely helps weight loss as part of a calorie-controlled or energy-controlled diet.

12.11   Advertisements for weight control or slimming products or services must not be targeted directly at individuals with a Body Mass Index of 30 or above (obesity) or use testimonials or case histories referring to subjects who were or seemed to be obese before using the advertised product.

  12.11.1   Advertisements for clinics or other establishments that offer treatment under suitably qualified medical supervision and advertisements for non-prescription medicines that are indicated for the treatment of obesity and that require the involvement of a pharmacist in the sale or supply of the medicine may nevertheless be targeted at those who are obese. Please see rule 11.9, "Services including Clinics, Establishments and the like Offering Advice on, or Treatment in, Medical, Personal or other Health Matters".

12.12   Advertisements for weight-control or slimming products must not suggest or imply that to be underweight is acceptable or desirable. If they are used, testimonials or case histories must not refer to subjects who are or seem to be underweight. Underweight, for the purpose of this rule, means a Body Mass Index below 20.

12.13   Advertisements for specially formulated products intended for use in energy-restricted diets that, when used as instructed by the manufacturer, replace the whole of the total daily diet or one or more meals of the daily diet must comply with the Foods Intended for Use in Energy Restricted Diets For Weight Reduction Regulations 1997 (as amended), specifically:

12.13.1   advertisements for such foods may not be offered under any name except "total diet replacement for weight control" or "meal replacement for weight control"

12.13.2   advertisements for such foods may not refer to the rate or amount of weight loss that could result from use of the product.

12.14   For the purposes of this rule, very low-calorie diets (VLCDs) are those with a daily intake of less than 800 kilo-calories. They must comply with the provisions of the Food Safety Act 1990 and relevant regulations made under it, including those on advertising. These conditions apply to advertisements for such products:

12.14.1   the advertisement must include a clear injunction to consult your doctor before embarking on the diet

12.14.2   the diet must be positioned as a short-term measure only

12.14.3   testimonials or specific case histories must not be used

12.14.4   independent medical advice must be sought on whether the proposed advertisement accords with the guidance on "Obesity: the prevention, identification, assessment and management of overweight and obesity in adults and children" (2006) published by the National Institute for Health and Clinical Excellence.

12.15   Advertisements for establishments offering weight-control or slimming treatments are acceptable only if they make clear that dietary control is necessary to achieve weight loss. An exception is made for clinics and other establishments that provide immediate weight loss surgery under suitably qualified medical supervision and are run in accordance with rule 11.9. Those clinics and establishments must not refer to the amount of weight that can be lost.

13

Food, food supplements and associated health or nutrition claims

Principle

Public health policy increasingly emphasises good dietary behaviour and an active lifestyle as a means of promoting health. Commercial product advertising cannot reasonably be expected to perform the same role as education and public information in promoting a varied and balanced diet but should not undermine progress towards national dietary improvement by misleading or confusing consumers or by setting a bad example, especially to children. The spirit, as well as the letter, of the rules in this section applies to all advertisements that promote, directly or indirectly, a food or soft drink product.

Background

These rules must be read in conjunction with the relevant legislation including the Food Safety Act 1990, the Food Labelling Regulations 1996 (as amended), especially Schedule 6 and Regulation (EC) No 1924/2006 on Nutrition and Health Claims made on Foods. They apply to all broadcast advertisements for food products.

Regulation (EC) No 1924/2006 on Nutrition and Health Claims made on Foods is complex and mandatory and seeks to protect consumers from misleading or false claims. Specific conditions of use associated with authorised health and nutrition claims are determined at a European level. Transitional periods apply and broadcasters are advised to take advice on the effect of the Regulation. Advertising industry stakeholders might find the Guidance to Compliance with European Regulation (EC) No 1924 on Nutrition and Health Claims Made on Foods published by the Food Standards Agency useful: www.food.gov.uk.

References to food apply also to soft drinks.

Rules

General

13.1   **Radio Central Copy Clearance –** Radio broadcasters must ensure advertisements subject to this Section are centrally cleared.

13.2   Advertisements must avoid anything likely to condone or encourage poor nutritional habits or an unhealthy lifestyle, especially in children.

   13.2.1   Advertisements must not condone or encourage damaging oral healthcare practices, especially in children.

13.3   Advertisements must not condone or encourage excessive consumption of any food.

13.4   Only nutrition claims listed in the Annex of Regulation 1924/2006 are permitted in advertisements.

Authorised health claims in the Community Register or claims that would have the same meaning for the audience may be used in advertisements:

www.ec.europa.eu/food/food/labellingnutrition/claims/community_register/authorised_health_claims_en.htm

Depending on the nature of the claim Regulation 1924/2006 contains a number of complex transitional periods, including those for health claims which are still being assessed for adoption to the EU list of permitted health claims (and which comply with existing national provisions) and for trade marks or brand names in use prior to 1 January 2005. There is no transition period for disease risk claims which are prohibited until authorised. BCAP advises advertising industry stakeholders to take advice on the effect of the Regulation.

13.4.1   Nutrition claims or claims that would have the same meaning for the audience, must comply with the criteria in the annex of Regulation 1924/2006. The Annex provisions can be found at:

www.ec.europa.eu/food/food/labellingnutrition/claims/community_register/nutrition_claims_en.htm

13.4.2   Advertisements that contain nutrition or health claims must be supported by documentary evidence to show they meet the conditions of use associated with the relevant claim. Advertisements must not give a misleading impression of the nutrition or health benefits of the product as a whole and factual nutrition statements should not imply a nutrition or health claim that cannot be supported. Claims must be presented clearly and without exaggeration

13.4.3   References to general benefits of a nutrient or food for overall good health or health-related well-being are acceptable only if accompanied by a relevant authorised claim

13.4.4   Claims of a nutrition or health benefit that gives rise to doubt the safety or nutritional adequacy of another product are unacceptable.

13.5   Comparisons between foods must not discourage the selection of options such as fresh fruit and fresh vegetables, which generally accepted dietary opinion recommends should form a greater part of the average diet. Advertisements must not disparage good dietary practice. No advertisement should suggest that a balanced and varied diet cannot provide adequate nutrients in general.

13.5.1   Comparative nutrition claims must compare the difference in the claimed nutrient to a range of foods of the same category which do not have the composition that allows them to bear a nutrition claim

---

13.5.2   An advertisement may use one product as the sole reference for comparison only if that product is representative of the products in its category

13.5.3   The difference in the quantity of a nutrient or energy value must be stated in the advertisement and must relate to the same quantity of food.

The European Commission has produced guidance on food categories that advertising industry stakeholders might find useful:

http://ec.europa.eu/food/food/labellingnutrition/claims/guidance_claim_14-12-07.pdf

13.6   These are not acceptable in advertisements for products subject to this section:

13.6.1   Claims that state or imply health could be affected by not consuming a food

13.6.2   Claims that state or imply a food prevents, treats or cures human disease. Reduction-of-disease-risk claims are acceptable if authorised by the European Commission

13.6.3   Health claims that refer to the recommendation of an individual health professional. Health claims that refer to the recommendation of an association are acceptable only if that association is a health-related charity or a national representative body of medicine, nutrition or dietetics

13.6.4   References to changes in bodily functions that could give rise to or exploit fear in the audience

13.6.5   Health claims that refer to a rate or amount of weight loss.

Vitamins, Minerals and Other Food Supplements

BCAP advises advertising industry stakeholders to ensure that claims made for vitamins, minerals and other food supplements are in line with the requirements of Regulation 1924/2006.

13.7   Advertisements must not state or imply that a balanced and varied diet cannot provide appropriate quantities of nutrients in general. Individuals must not be encouraged to swap a healthy diet for supplementation.

13.7.1   Nutrition and health claims for food supplements must be permitted or authorised as provided for at rule 13.4 above. Advertisements that contain Nutrition or health claims must be supported by documentary evidence to show they meet the conditions of use associated with the relevant claim, as specified by the European Commission.

Infant and Follow-on Formula

These rules must be read in conjunction with the relevant legislation including the Infant Formula and Follow-on Formula Regulations 2007 (as amended) and the Regulation 1924/2006.

13.8   Advertisements for infant formula are prohibited.

13.8.1   Advertisements must not confuse between infant formula and follow-on formula.

Food and Soft Drink Product Advertising to Children

Background

These rules should be read in conjunction with the general rules in this section and other rules in this code, especially Section 5: Children and, for television only, Section 32: Scheduling.

The spirit, as well as the letter, of the rules in this section applies to all advertisements that promote, directly or indirectly, a food.

Definitions

"Children": persons below the age of 16.

"Advertisements targeted directly at pre-school or primary school children": advertisements that directly target pre-school or primary school children through their content as opposed to their scheduling. For rules on the scheduling of HFSS product advertisements, please see Section 32: Scheduling.

"Equity brand characters": those characters that have been created by the advertiser and have no separate identity outside their associated product or brand.

"Licensed characters": those characters that are borrowed equities and have no historical association with the product.

"HFSS products": those food or drink products that are assessed as High in Fat, Salt or Sugar in accordance with the nutrient profiling scheme published by the Food Standards Agency (FSA) on 6 December 2005. Information on the FSA's nutrient profiling scheme is available on the FSA website at:

www.food.gov.uk/healthiereating/advertisingtochildren/nutlab/nutprofmod

For the avoidance of doubt, HFSS product advertisements may make nutritional or health claims in accordance with rule 13.4.

References to food apply also to soft drinks.

13.9   **Television only** – Promotional offers must be used with a due sense of responsibility. They may not be used in HFSS product advertisements targeted directly at pre-school or primary school children.

> **13.9.1**   Advertisements featuring a promotional offer linked to a food product of interest to children must avoid creating a sense of urgency or encouraging the purchase of an excessive quantity for irresponsible consumption
>
> **13.9.2**   Advertisements must not seem to encourage children to eat or drink a product only to take advantage of a promotional offer: the product should be offered on its merits, with the offer as an added incentive. Advertisements featuring a promotional offer should ensure a significant presence for the product
>
> **13.9.3**   Advertisements for collection-based promotions must not seem to urge children or their parents to buy excessive quantities of food. They must not directly encourage children only to collect promotional items, emphasise the number of items to be collected or create a sense of urgency. If a promotional offer can also be bought, that must be made clear. Closing dates for collection-based promotions must enable the whole set to be collected without having to buy excessive or irresponsible quantities of the product in a short time
>
> **13.9.4**   Advertisements must not encourage children to eat more than they otherwise would.
>
> The notion of excessive or irresponsible consumption relates to the frequency of consumption as well as the amount consumed.

13.10   **Television only** – Licensed characters and celebrities popular with children must be used with a due sense of responsibility. They may not be used in HFSS product advertisements targeted directly at pre-school or primary school children.

That prohibition does not apply to advertiser-created equity brand characters (puppets, persons or characters), which may be used by advertisers to sell the products they were designed to sell.

Licensed characters and celebrities popular with children may present factual and relevant generic statements about nutrition, safety, education or similar.

13.11   **Television only** – No nutrition or health claim may be used in HFSS product advertisements targeted directly at pre-school or primary school children. For the avoidance of doubt, claims referring to children's development or health are acceptable in non-HFSS product advertisements, if those claims are authorised by the European Commission.

13.12   **Television only** – Although children might be expected to exercise some preference over the food they eat or drink, advertisements must be prepared with a due sense of responsibility and must not directly advise or ask children to buy or to ask their parents or other adults to make enquiries or purchases for them. (Please see rule 5.9 in Section 5: Children)

13.12.1   Nothing in an advertisement may seem to encourage children to pester or make a nuisance of themselves

13.12.2   Advertisements must not imply that children will be inferior to others, disloyal or will have let someone down, if they or their family do not buy, consume or use a product or service

13.12.3   Advertisements must neither try to sell to children by appealing to emotions such as pity, fear, loyalty or self-confidence nor suggest that having the advertised product somehow confers superiority, for example, making a child more confident, clever, popular or successful

13.12.4   Advertisements addressed to children must not urge children to buy or persuade others to buy and must avoid high-pressure or hard-sell techniques. Neither the words used nor the tone of the advertisement should suggest that young viewers could be bullied, cajoled or otherwise put under pressure to acquire the advertised item

13.12.5   If an advertisement for a children's product contains a price, the price must not be minimised by the use of words such as "only" or "just".

13.13   **Radio only** – Promotional offers to children must be used with a due sense of responsibility. They may not be used in food or soft drink product advertisements targeted directly at pre-school or primary school children; that prohibition does not apply to advertisements for fresh fruit or fresh vegetables. Advertisements that contain a promotional offer linked to a food or drink product of interest to children must neither seem to encourage children to eat or drink a product only to take advantage of a promotional offer nor create a sense of urgency. If a promotional item can also be bought, that must be made clear. Closing dates for collection-based promotions must enable the whole set to be collected without having to buy excessive or irresponsible quantities of the product in a short time.

13.14   **Radio only –** Licensed characters and celebrities popular with children must be used with a due sense of responsibility. They may not be used in food or soft drink product advertisements targeted directly at pre-school or primary school children. That prohibition does not apply to advertisements for fresh fruit or fresh vegetables or to advertiser-created equity brand characters (puppets, persons or characters), which may be used by advertisers to sell the products they were designed to sell.

Licensed characters, equity brand characters or celebrities well-known to children may present factual and relevant generic statements about nutrition, safety, education and the like.

13.15   **Radio only –** Claims referring to children's development or health are acceptable in radio food or soft drink product advertisements if those claims are authorised by the European Commission.

14

Financial products, services and investments

Background

The rules in this section largely draw attention to statutory regulation with which all advertisements must comply. Selecting the most relevant financial products or services normally requires consumers to consider many factors; short-form television and radio advertisements are not well-suited to communicating large amounts of detail. They are not, therefore, suitable formats for advertising especially high-risk or specialist investments or any financial products or services that are not regulated or permitted in the UK under the Financial Services and Markets Act 2000 (FSMA).

The ASA and BCAP Executive may seek advice from other regulators when investigating possible breaches of the BCAP Code. They will apply their usual standards to prevent misleading advertising (see Section 3: Misleading Advertising) and require significant exceptions and qualifications to be made clear (see rule 3.10). The *Financial Services Authority (FSA) Handbook* requires financial promotions to be "fair, clear and not misleading".

Definitions

In this section, unless otherwise stated, the terms "financial promotion", "authorised person", "qualifying credit" and "regulated activity" have the same meanings as in FSMA and the Financial Services and Markets Act (Financial Promotion) Order 2005 (FPO) (as amended). The FSMA definition of a financial promotion is broad and includes, for example, advertisements for deposits and insurance products.

Under FSMA, a financial promotion is "an invitation or inducement to engage in investment activity" that is made "in the course of business" and is "capable of having an effect in the UK." That broad definition captures all promotional activity, including traditional advertising, telephone sales and face-to-face conversations, in relation to all products and services regulated by the FSA. Under FSMA, "investment activity" does not cover only conventional investments; it includes deposits, home finance transactions (regulated mortgages, home purchase plans and home reversion plans), other forms of secured credit and most insurance, including some advertisements by insurance intermediaries (see the Insurance Conduct of Business sourcebook – ICOBS).

The FSA is the regulator for the financial services industry and regulates conduct of business, including advertising, for investment products, including structured deposits where capital is subject to market risk. It also regulates the advertising of insurance, including the activities of insurance intermediaries (for example motor, home and travel insurers). It is responsible for the regulation of most first-charge mortgage lending and selling. Mortgages that are not regulated are those secured on non-UK land and business premises with less than 40% residential occupation. The FSA's financial promotion rules set out in *Mortgages and Home Finance: Conduct of Business* sourcebook (MCOB) Chapter 3 in the *FSA Handbook* apply to Home Reversion Plans, sale and rent back business and qualifying credit promotions as defined under the FPO and the *FSA Handbook* glossary. The rules in MCOB 3 do not apply to Home Purchase Plans, with the exception of the fair, clear and not misleading standard and some relevant guidance detailed in MCOB Chapter 2.

Unsecured lending, other forms of secured lending and some other credit activities continue to be regulated by the Consumer Credit Act 1974 (as amended) and the Consumer Credit (Advertisements) Regulations 2004 (as amended).

The FSA regulates the activity of accepting deposits from banking customers in the UK under the Banking Conduct Regime, which applies the FSA's Principles for Businesses, the conduct of business requirements of the Payment Services Regulations (PSRs) and the *Banking Conduct of Business* sourcebook (BCOBS). BCOBS Chapter 2 states that, when designing a financial promotion, a firm may find it helpful to take account of the British Bankers' Association/Building Societies' Association Code of Conduct for the Advertising of Interest Bearing Accounts.

A "specialised financial channel or station" is an Ofcom-licensed channel or station whose programmes, with few exceptions, are likely to be of particular interest only to business people or finance professionals.

In this Code, "spread betting" and "contract for differences" have the same meanings as in the glossary to the *FSA Handbook*.

Rules

14.1   **Radio Central Copy Clearance –** Radio broadcasters must ensure advertisements for consumer credit, investment and complex financial products and services are centrally cleared.

14.2   Broadcasters are responsible for ensuring that advertisements carried by them comply with all the relevant legal and regulatory requirements. Broadcasters might need to seek legal advice if an advertiser claims an advertisement should be considered:

    14.2.1   not to be a financial promotion or

    14.2.2   to be a financial promotion that is not required to be communicated or approved by an authorised person (because it is subject to an exemption under the FPO).

        Advice, or general advice from the FSA, might be required on compliance with the *FSA Handbook*. The FSA does not pre-vet or advise on the compliance of proposed financial promotions with FSMA. For more information, visit the financial promotions pages of the FSA website (www.fsa.gov.uk) and see the *FSA Handbook*, especially the *Conduct of Business* sourcebook (COBS) Chapter 4, MCOB Chapter 3, ICOBS Chapter 2.2 and the *Perimeter Guidance Manual* (PERG) Chapter 8.

14.3   Advertisements for financial services that are broadcast exclusively to audiences in EU Member States other than the UK or are not subject to the FSA's financial promotion rules need not comply with this section. Instead, they must comply with the laws and regulations of the relevant Member States.

14.4   Financial promotions or other advertisements for regulated activities may be broadcast if:

     14.4.1   communicated by an authorised person

     14.4.2   approved or issued by an authorised person or an appointed representative of an authorised person who, to the broadcaster's satisfaction, has confirmed that the final recorded version of the advertisement complies with the FSA's financial promotion rules or

     14.4.3   exempt under the FPO. An advertisement by a general insurance intermediary need not be approved by an authorised person if it is a generic promotion and exempted by the FPO. (That is usually if the advertisement does not identify an insurer, insurance intermediary or product; so it will usually apply if the financial promotion refers generally to product types.)

14.5   These categories of advertisement may be broadcast on specialised financial channels, stations or programming only:

     14.5.1   advertisements for the acquisition or disposal of derivatives, warrants or other transferable securities (such as shares) that are not on the Official List of the FSA or admitted to trading on a Regulated Market in the UK or other EEA State (as defined by the Markets in Financial Instruments Directive)

     14.5.2   advertisements for spread betting, as an investment only. Spread betting advertisements may be advertised on interactive or additional TV services (including text services). They must comply with the gambling rules (see Section 17: Gambling. The advertised products or services should be available only to clients who have demonstrated through a pre-vetting procedure compliant with the FSA's appropriateness test that they have relevant financial trading experience

     14.5.3   advertisements for contracts for differences (except spread betting), provided the products are available only to clients who have demonstrated through an appropriate pre-vetting procedure that they have relevant financial trading experience.

     14.5.4   advertisements for investments not regulated or permitted under FSMA. An advertisement that implies, for example, that a collectors' item or other unregulated product or service could have investment potential (in the colloquial sense) would normally be unacceptable.

14.6   Unless they are obviously addressed to a specialist audience and shown either on specialised financial channels or stations or in breaks in relevant financial programmes, advertisements subject to this section must be considered to be addressed to non-specialist audiences. No specialist knowledge should normally be required for a clear understanding of claims or references. For example, exceptions, conditions or expressions that would be understood by finance specialists must be avoided or explained if they would be unfamiliar to the audience.

14.7   References to interest payable on savings are acceptable, subject to these conditions:

    14.7.1   they must be factually accurate at the time of broadcast and the advertisement must be modified immediately if the rate changes

    14.7.2   advertisements quoting a rate must use the Annual Equivalent Rate (AER) and the contractual rate as set out in the British Bankers' Association and Building Societies Association Code of Conduct for the Advertising of Interest Bearing Accounts and advertisements should comply with all the provisions of that code

    14.7.3   if conditions apply to calculations of interest and might affect the sum received, the advertisement must refer to the conditions and how they can be accessed

    14.7.4   advertisements quoting a rate must make clear whether it is gross or net of tax, or tax-free, but do not need to explain those expressions

    14.7.5   where the interest rate is variable, this must be stated

    14.7.6   if the investment returns of different types of savings products are compared (for example, a unit trust and a bank deposit), significant differences between the products must be explained.

14.8   Subject to legal requirements, reference to specific sums assured in life insurance advertisements must be accompanied by all relevant qualifying conditions; for example, age and gender of the assured at the outset of the policy, period of policy and amount and number of premiums payable.

14.9   References to income tax and other tax benefits must be properly qualified, clarifying their meaning and making clear, if relevant, that the tax treatment depends on the individual circumstances of each person and could be subject to change in future.

Lending and Credit

14.10   Advertisements for paper or electronic publications (for example, periodicals, books and text services) must not recommend a specific investment offer.

14.11   The advertising of consumer credit or hire services is acceptable only if the advertiser complies with the Consumer Credit (Advertisements) Regulations 2004 (as amended) and the Consumer Credit Act 1974 (as amended). Credit advertisements that are not qualifying credit promotions must comply with Section 46 of the Consumer Credit Act and Regulations made under it. If the applicability or interpretation of those Regulations is in doubt, advertisers must be encouraged to seek guidance from their Local Trading Standards department. Such advertisements that involve distance marketing must also comply with the Financial Services (Distance Marketing) Regulations 2004. Other distance-marketing financial advertisements are covered by the *FSA Handbook*. Similarly, qualifying credit promotions and sale and rent back promotions must comply with the requirements imposed by FSMA and MCOB. The advertising of home finance transactions (regulated mortgages, home purchase plans and home reversion plans) regulated by the FSA is acceptable only if the advertiser complies with the FSMA and the *FSA Handbook*.

14.12   Advertisements for mortgages and re-mortgages are normally financial promotions under FSMA and must comply with the requirements imposed by FSMA and MCOB.

   14.12.1   Advertisements for most loans secured by a second charge are credit advertisements and the requirements of the Consumer Credit (Advertisements) Regulations 2004 (as amended) therefore apply. Special note should be taken of the requirements in those Regulations for secured loans

   14.12.2   Advertisements for some mortgages might also have to comply with the provisions of COBS (for example if an investment product is being sold alongside a mortgage).

14.13   Advertising for debt management services is acceptable only from bodies that:

   14.13.1   are licensed under the Consumer Credit Act 1974 (as amended) and

   14.13.2   undertake to comply with the Debt Management Guidance published by the Office of Fair Trading.

Direct remittance

14.14   Advertisements on television or radio are unacceptable if they directly or indirectly invite the remittance of money direct to the advertiser or any other person without offering an opportunity to receive more information; an intermediate stage at which more information is supplied is mandatory.

14.15   Advertisements on Ofcom-regulated text services that invite the direct remittance of money are acceptable for the categories listed in rule 14.4, but not those in rule 14.5.

15

Faith, religion and equivalent systems of belief

Principle

These rules seek to strike a balance between freedom of speech and the prevention of advertising that could be harmful. BCAP intends them to:

- **reduce the social harm that can result from damage to inter-faith relations**
- **protect the young and allow parents to exercise choice in their children's moral and philosophical education**
- **protect those who are vulnerable because, for example, of sickness or bereavement**
- **prevent potentially harmful advertisements from exploiting their audience.**

Definitions

The rules in this section apply to:

- advertisements, about any matter, by or on behalf of bodies that are wholly or mainly concerned with religion, faith or other systems of belief that can reasonably be regarded as equivalent to those that involve recognition of a deity, including belief in the non-existence of deities
- advertisements, by any body, that wholly or mainly concern matters of religion, faith or equivalent systems of belief
- advertisements, by any body, for products or services related to such matters.
- some advertisements subject to this Section are also subject to Section 7: Political and Controversial Matters or Section 16: Charities.

Rules

15.1   **Radio Central Copy Clearance –** Radio advertisements subject to this section must be centrally cleared.

15.2   Broadcasters must not accept advertisements from or on behalf of bodies:

      15.2.1   that practise or advocate illegal behaviour or

      15.2.2   whose rites or other forms of collective observance are not normally directly accessible to the general public or

      15.2.3   that apply unreasonable pressure on people to join or participate or not to opt out.

15.3   Broadcasters must be satisfied that no representatives will contact respondents without their consent.

15.4   Television advertisements must not promote psychic practices or practices related to the occult, except those permitted by rule 15.5. Radio advertisements may promote psychic and occult practices but must not make efficacy claims.

Psychic and occult-related practices include ouija, satanism, casting of spells palmistry, attempts to contact the dead, divination, clairvoyance, clairaudience, the invocation of spirits or demons and exorcism.

15.5   **Television only –** Subject to rules 15.5.1 and 15.5.2, television advertisements may promote services that the audience is likely to regard merely as entertainment and that offer generalised advice that would obviously be applicable to a large section of the population, for example, typical newspaper horoscopes.

15.5.1   Advertisements may promote a pre-recorded tarot-based prediction service if:

15.5.1.a   the service includes no content that respondents might feel to be threatening and

15.5.1.b   both the advertisement and the service state clearly that the service is pre-recorded and qualify references to "tarot" to make clear that the predictions are not based on live readings.

15.5.2   Advertisements for personalised and live services that rely on belief in astrology, horoscopes, tarot and derivative practices are acceptable only on channels that are licensed for the purpose of the promotion of such services and are appropriately labelled: both the advertisement and the product or service itself must state that the product or service is for entertainment purposes only.

15.5.3   Advertising permitted under rule 15.5 may not:

- Make claims for efficacy or accuracy;
- Predict negative experiences or specific events;
- Offer life-changing advice directed at individuals – including advice related to health (including pregnancy) or financial situation;
- Appeal particularly to children;
- Encourage excessive use.

15.6   Advertisements must identify the advertiser and its faith, if that is not obvious from the context.

15.7   Television and television text advertisements must not expound doctrines or beliefs, unless they are broadcast on channels whose editorial content is wholly or mainly concerned with matters of religion, faith or equivalent systems of belief ("specialist broadcasters"). Advertisements carried by specialist broadcasters may express the advertiser's opinion on matters of doctrine or belief but must not present it as unqualified fact and must make clear to the audience that it is the advertiser's opinion.

Radio advertisements may expound doctrines or beliefs if they are presented as the advertiser's opinion.

15.8   Advertisements must not exhort audience members to change their beliefs or behaviour.

15.9   Advertisements must not refer to the alleged consequences of faith or lack of faith. They must not present the advertiser's beliefs as the "one" or "true" faith.

15.10   Advertisements must not denigrate the beliefs of others.

15.11   Advertisements must not appeal for funds, except for charitable purposes. If the charitable purpose includes or will be accompanied by recruitment or evangelism, the advertisement must make that clear.

Before broadcasting an advertisement that includes a charitable appeal, broadcasters must seek to be satisfied that the funds raised will be used solely for the benefit of specified groups.

Advertisements must not imply that respondents will receive spiritual benefits in return for a donation to the advertised cause.

15.12   Advertisements must not exploit the hopes or fears of the vulnerable. The elderly, the sick and the bereaved should be regarded as especially vulnerable.

15.13   Advertisements must not claim that faith healing, miracle working or faith-based counselling can treat, cure or alleviate physical or mental health problems; they may, however, make restrained and proportionate claims that such services can benefit emotional or spiritual well-being.

15.14   Advertisements must not appeal particularly to people under 18 and must not be broadcast during or adjacent to programmes that appeal or are likely to appeal particularly to those under 18.

This rule does not apply to advertisements for public events, including services and festivals, that children are likely to participate in or to advertisements for publications or similar merchandise that are designed for children, provided that neither the advertisement nor the advertised product or service is linked to recruitment or fund-raising. It does not apply to advertisements on channels or stations whose editorial content is dedicated to matters of religion, faith or equivalent systems of belief.

15.15   Advertisements must not feature children as presenters, unless the advertisement is for an event, such as Christmas carol services or Diwali celebrations, that children are especially likely to take part in.

16
Charities

Principle

These rules are intended to prevent the abuse of people's charitable impulses. Charity advertisements or advertisements that feature charities should treat with care and discretion any subjects likely to arouse strong emotions. Although audiences are generally more tolerant of potentially distressing treatments when the objectives of an advertisement are charitable, sensitivity is nevertheless required especially in relation to younger audiences.

Background

If it is relevant, broadcasters should take care to comply with Section 5: Children, Section 7: Political and Controversial Matters, Section 9: Environmental Claims, Section 15: Faith, Religion and Equivalent Systems of Belief, and Section 32: Scheduling.

Advertisements must comply with the requirements of the Charities Act 1993 (as amended) and all relevant data protection legislation. For information on the Data Protection Act 1998 go to: www.ico.gov.uk

Definitions

Rules in this section regulate charity advertisements and not the charities themselves, which are regulated by the Charity Commission (England and Wales) www.charitycommission.gov.uk, The Department for Social Development (Northern Ireland) www.dsdni.gov.uk, and the Office of the Scottish Charity Regulator (Scotland) www.oscr.org.uk.

The rules apply to advertisements for charities (which include charitable bodies) and advertisements for other products and services that promote the needs or objectives of charities.

Rules

16.1 **Radio Central Copy Clearance –** Radio broadcasters must ensure advertisements subject to this section are centrally cleared.

16.2 Advertising is acceptable only from:

16.2.1 bodies registered with the relevant UK authorities as having charitable status or bodies that have had their charitable status otherwise officially recognised, for example by HM Revenue & Customs: www.hmrc.gov.uk/index.htm.

16.2.2   bodies based outside the UK that supply to broadcasters confirmation that they comply with all relevant legislation in their home countries and evidence of their good faith, which might include audited accounts and a list of members of their governing body.

16.3   Advertisements seeking donations for, or promoting the needs or objectives of a charitable body must not:

16.3.1   misrepresent the body, its activities or the benefits of donated funds or exaggerate the scale or nature of the cause it claims to support

16.3.2   suggest that anyone will lack proper feeling or fail in a responsibility by not supporting a charity

16.3.3   disrespect the dignity of those on whose behalf an appeal is being made

16.3.4   address fund-raising messages to children or likely to be of particular interest to them.

16.4   If the advertisement states that payment may be made by credit or debit card, the donor's right to have any payment of £100 or more refunded must be stated.

Rules that apply to references to charities in other advertisements

16.5   Advertisements by non-charity advertisers which promote the needs or objects of charitable bodies, or offer to assist them, are only acceptable if the bodies would be acceptable advertisers in their own right under rule 16.2.

16.6   Advertisements that include an offer to donate money to charity must:

16.6.1   not depend on sales reaching a given level or be subject to a similar condition. If a target total or an amount for each purchase is stated, any extra money given to the charity must be donated on the same basis as contributions below that level

16.6.2   identify the charity that will benefit and state the basis on which the contribution will be calculated (in accordance with rule 16.9) and, where more than one charity is involved, the advertisement may give a generic identification but should be accompanied by a statement listing the charities and the proportions in which they will benefit.

16.7   Broadcasters must hold evidence that each charity has agreed to the proposed advertisement.

16.8   Advertisements for medicinal products may offer to donate money to charity but must not be likely to encourage indiscriminate, unnecessary or excessive purchases of medicinal products. Advertisements must state the basis on which the contribution will be calculated.

See also Section 11: Medicines, Medical Devices, Treatments and Health

16.9   Where a promotion states or implies that part of the price paid for goods or services will be given to a charity or cause, the advertisement must state the actual amount or percentage of the price that will be paid to the charity or cause, for example, "£1 per sale" or "10% of the purchase price".

       16.9.1   For any other promotion linked to a charity or where a third party states or implies that donations will be given to a charity or cause, the advertisement must state the total (or a reasonable estimate) of the amount the charity or cause will receive.

17
Gambling

Principle

The rules in this section are designed to ensure that gambling advertisements are socially responsible, with particular regard to the need to protect under-18s and other vulnerable persons from being harmed or exploited by advertising that features or promotes gambling.

Background

The Gambling Act 2005 does not apply outside Great Britain. Licensees should ensure that specialist legal advice is sought when considering advertising any gambling product or service in Northern Ireland or the Channel Islands.

Spread betting may be advertised as an investment activity under the Financial Services and Markets Act (FSMA) 2000, the Financial Services and Markets Act 2000 (Financial Promotion) Order 2005 (as amended) and in accordance with the *FSA Handbook*. Spread betting may be advertised on specialised financial stations or channels, in specialised financial programming or on interactive or additional television services (including text services) only (see rule 14.5.4). A "spread bet" is a contract for differences that is a gaming contract, as defined in the glossary to the *FSA Handbook*.

These rules are not intended to inhibit advertisements to counter problem gambling that are responsible and unlikely to promote a brand or type of gambling.

Please refer to Section 32: Scheduling for rules on the scheduling of gambling advertisements.

Definitions

The term "gambling" means gaming and betting, as defined in the Gambling Act 2005, and spread betting. For rules on lottery advertisements, see Section 18.

The rules in this section apply to advertisements for "play for money" gambling products and advertisements for "play for free" gambling products that offer the chance to win a prize or that explicitly or implicitly direct the consumer to a "play for money" gambling product, whether on-shore or off-shore.

Unless they portray or refer to gambling, this section does not apply to advertisements for non-gambling leisure events or facilities, for example, hotels, cinemas, bowling alleys or ice rinks, that are in the same complex as, but separate from, gambling events or facilities.

Rules

17.1	**Radio Central Copy Clearance** – Radio broadcasters must ensure that advertisements for gambling are centrally cleared.
17.2	Advertisements for events or facilities that can be accessed only by entering gambling premises must make that condition clear.

Rules for all advertisements

17.3   Advertisements must not:

17.3.1   portray, condone or encourage gambling behaviour that is socially irresponsible or could lead to financial, social or emotional harm

17.3.2   suggest that gambling can provide an escape from personal, professional or educational problems such as loneliness or depression

17.3.3   suggest that gambling can be a solution to financial concerns, an alternative to employment or a way to achieve financial security

17.3.4   portray gambling as indispensable or as taking priority in life; for example, over family, friends or professional or educational commitments

17.3.5   suggest peer pressure to gamble or disparage abstention

17.3.6   suggest that gambling can enhance personal qualities; for example, that it can improve self-image or self-esteem, or is a way to gain control, superiority, recognition or admiration

17.3.7   link gambling to seduction, sexual success or enhanced attractiveness

17.3.8   portray gambling in a context of toughness or link it to resilience or recklessness

17.3.9   suggest gambling is a rite of passage

17.3.10   suggest that solitary gambling is preferable to social gambling.

Rules for gambling advertisements

17.4   Advertisements for gambling must not:

17.4.1   exploit cultural beliefs or traditions about gambling or luck

17.4.2   condone or encourage criminal or anti-social behaviour

17.4.3   condone or feature gambling in a working environment (an exception exists for licensed gambling premises)

17.4.4   exploit the susceptibilities, aspirations, credulity, inexperience or lack of knowledge of under-18s or other vulnerable persons

17.4.5   be likely to be of particular appeal to under-18s, especially by reflecting or being associated with youth culture

17.4.6   feature anyone who is, or seems to be, under 25 years old gambling or playing a significant role. No-one may behave in an adolescent, juvenile or loutish way.

17.5   Advertisements for family entertainment centres, travelling fairs, horse racecourses and dog racetracks, and for non-gambling leisure facilities that incidentally refer to separate gambling facilities as part of a list of facilities on, for example, a cruise ship, may include under-18s provided they are accompanied by an adult and are socialising responsibly in areas that the Gambling Act 2005 does not restrict by age.

18
Lotteries

Principle

The rules in this section are designed to ensure that lottery advertisements are socially responsible, with particular regard to the need to protect under-18s and other vulnerable persons from being harmed or exploited by advertisements that feature or promote lotteries.

Background

This section applies to advertisements for lottery products that are licensed and regulated by the Gambling Commission, the National Lottery Commission, or in the case of small society lotteries, registered with local authorities in England and Wales or licensing boards in Scotland.

The UK National Lottery may be advertised under The National Lottery etc Act 1993 and The National Lottery Regulations 1994 (as amended). Advertisements for the UK National Lottery are subject to the National Lottery Advertising and Sales Promotion Code of Practice, approved by the National Lottery Commission.

Rules

18.1   **Radio Central Copy Clearance –** Radio broadcasters must ensure that advertisements subject to this section are centrally cleared.

Rules for all advertisements

18.2   Advertisements must not:

18.2.1   portray, condone or encourage gambling behaviour that is socially irresponsible or could lead to financial, social or emotional harm

18.2.2   suggest that participating in a lottery can provide an escape from personal, professional or educational problems such as loneliness or depression

18.2.3   suggest that participating in a lottery can be a solution to financial concerns, an alternative to employment or a way to achieve financial security. Advertisers may, however, refer to other benefits of winning a prize

18.2.4   portray participating in a lottery as indispensable or as taking priority in life, for example, over family, friends or professional or educational commitments

18.2.5   suggest peer pressure to participate in a lottery or disparage abstention

18.2.6   suggest that participating in a lottery can enhance personal qualities; for example, that it can improve self-image or self-esteem, or is a way to gain control, superiority, recognition or admiration

18.2.7   link participating in a lottery to seduction, sexual success or enhanced attractiveness

18.2.8   not portray participation in a lottery in a context of toughness or link it to resilience or recklessness

18.2.9   suggest participation in a lottery is a rite of passage

18.2.10   suggest that solitary gambling is preferable to social gambling.

Rules for lottery advertisements

18.3   Advertisements for lotteries that can be participated in only by entering gambling premises must make that condition clear.

18.4   Advertisements for lotteries must not exploit the susceptibilities, aspirations, credulity, inexperience or lack of knowledge of under-18s or other vulnerable persons.

18.5   Advertisements for lotteries must not be likely to be of particular appeal to under-18s, especially by reflecting or being associated with youth culture. Please refer to Section 32 for scheduling restrictions.

18.6   Advertisements for lotteries may include under-18s. No-one who is, or seems to be, under 25 years old may be featured gambling or playing a significant role.

18.7   Advertisements that exclusively feature the good causes that benefit from a lottery and include no explicit encouragement to buy a lottery product may include under-18s in a significant role.

18.8   Advertisements for lotteries must not exploit cultural beliefs or traditions about gambling or luck.

18.9   Advertisements for lotteries must not condone or encourage criminal or anti-social behaviour.

18.10   Advertisements for lotteries must not condone or feature gambling in a working environment (an exception exists for workplace lottery syndicates and gambling premises).

19

Alcohol

Principle

Advertisements for alcoholic drinks should not be targeted at people under 18 years of age and should not imply, condone or encourage immoderate, irresponsible or anti-social drinking.

The spirit as well as the letter of the rules in this section applies.

Definitions

The rules in this section apply to advertisements for alcoholic drinks and advertisements that feature or refer to alcoholic drinks. Alcoholic drinks are defined as those containing at least 0.5% alcohol; for the purposes of this Code low-alcohol drinks are defined as drinks containing between 0.5% and 1.2% alcohol.

Where stated, exceptions are made for low-alcohol drinks. But, if an advertisement for a low-alcohol drink could be considered to promote a stronger alcoholic drink or if the low-alcohol content of a drink is not stated clearly in the advertisement, all the rules in this section apply.

If a soft drink is promoted as a mixer, the rules in this section apply in full.

The rules are not intended to inhibit responsible advertisements that are intended to counter problem drinking or tell consumers about alcohol-related health or safety themes. Those advertisements should not be likely to promote an alcohol product or brand.

Rules

19.1   **Radio Central Copy Clearance –** Radio broadcasters must ensure advertisements for alcoholic drinks are centrally cleared.

Rules that apply to all advertisements

19.2   Advertisements must not feature, imply, condone or encourage irresponsible or immoderate drinking. That applies to both the amount of drink and the way drinking is portrayed.

           References to, or suggestions of, buying repeat rounds of alcoholic drinks are not acceptable. That does not prevent, for example, someone buying a drink for each member of a group. It does, however, prevent any suggestion that other members of the group will buy a round.

19.3   Advertisements must neither imply that alcohol can contribute to an individual's popularity or confidence nor imply that alcohol can enhance personal qualities.

19.4   Advertisements must not imply that drinking alcohol is a key component of social success or acceptance or that refusal is a sign of weakness. Advertisements must not imply that the success of a social occasion depends on the presence or consumption of alcohol.

19.5   Advertisements must not link alcohol with daring, toughness, aggression or unruly, irresponsible or antisocial behaviour.

19.6   Advertisements must not link alcohol with sexual activity, sexual success or seduction or imply that alcohol can enhance attractiveness. That does not preclude linking alcohol with romance or flirtation.

19.7   Advertisements must not portray alcohol as indispensable or as taking priority in life. Advertisements must not imply that drinking can overcome problems or that regular solitary drinking is acceptable.

19.8   Advertisements must not imply that alcohol has therapeutic qualities. Alcohol must not be portrayed as capable of changing mood, physical condition or behaviour or as a source of nourishment. Although they may refer to refreshment, advertisements must not imply that alcohol can improve any type of performance.

19.9   Advertisements must not link alcohol to illicit drugs.

19.10   Advertisements may give factual information about the alcoholic strength of a drink. They may also make a factual alcohol strength comparison with another product, but only when the comparison is with a higher strength product of a similar beverage.

Advertisements must not imply that a drink may be preferred because of its alcohol content or intoxicating effect. There is an exception for low-alcohol drinks, which may be presented as preferable because of their low alcoholic strength.

In the case of a drink with relatively high alcoholic strength in relation to its category, the factual information should not be given undue emphasis.

19.11   Advertisements may include alcohol sales promotions but must not imply, condone or encourage immoderate drinking.

19.12   Advertisements must not feature alcohol being handled or served irresponsibly.

19.13   Advertisements must not link alcohol with the use of potentially dangerous machinery or driving.

Advertisements may feature sporting and other physical activities (subject to other rules in this section) but must not imply that those activities have been undertaken after the consumption of alcohol.

19.14   Advertisements must not normally show alcohol being drunk by anyone in their working environment.

Rules that apply to alcohol advertisements

19.15   **Television only –** Alcohol advertisements must not:

     19.15.1   be likely to appeal strongly to people under 18, especially by reflecting or being associated with youth culture or showing adolescent or juvenile behaviour

     19.15.2   include a person or character whose example is likely to be followed by those aged under 18 years or who has a strong appeal to those aged under 18.

19.16   **Radio only –** Alcohol advertisements must not:

     19.16.1   be targeted at those under 18 years or use a treatment likely to be of particular appeal to them.

     19.16.2   include a person or character whose example is likely to be followed by those aged under 18 years or who has a particular appeal to those aged under 18.

19.17   Alcohol advertisements must not feature in a significant role anyone who is, or seems to be, under 25 and must not feature children.

An exception is made for advertisements that feature families socialising responsibly. Here, children may be included but they should have an incidental role only and anyone who seems to be under the age of 25 must be obviously not drinking alcohol.

19.18   Advertisements for alcoholic drinks may give factual statements about product contents, including comparisons, but must not make any health claims, which include fitness or weight-control claims.

The only permitted nutrition claims are "low alcohol", "reduced alcohol" and "reduced energy" and any claim likely to have the same meaning for the audience.

20
Motoring

Principle

Advertisements should not contribute to a culture of dangerous, irresponsible or inconsiderate driving or motorcycling, especially among young drivers.

Definition

"Motoring advertisements" are broadcast advertisements for vehicles or other automotive products; for example, tyres, fuel or car accessories. These rules do not apply to public service advertisements about road safety.

Rules

Rules for all advertisements:

20.1   Advertisements must not condone or encourage dangerous, competitive, inconsiderate or irresponsible driving or motorcycling. Advertisements must not suggest that driving or motorcycling safely is staid or boring.

20.2   Advertisements must not condone or encourage a breach of the legal requirements of the Highway Code.

Rules for motoring advertisements:

20.3   Motoring advertisements must not demonstrate power, acceleration or handling characteristics except in a clear context of safety. Reference to those characteristics must not suggest excitement, aggression or competitiveness.

20.4   Motoring advertisements must not refer to speed in a way that might condone or encourage dangerous, competitive, inconsiderate or irresponsible driving or motorcycling. Factual statements about a vehicle's speed or acceleration are permissible but must not be presented as a reason for preferring the advertised vehicle. Speed or acceleration claims must not be the main selling message of an advertisement.

20.5   Motoring advertisements must not exaggerate the benefit of safety features to consumers or suggest that a vehicle's features enable it to be driven or ridden faster or in complete safety.

21

Betting tipsters

Principle

Advertisements for betting tipster services should not be likely to mislead the audience.

Definition

"Proofing" means provably lodging and securely recording a betting tip with an independent and suitably qualified third party, such as a solicitor, before the start of the event to which the tip relates.

Rules

21.1	**Radio Central Copy Clearance** – Radio advertisements for betting tipsters must be centrally cleared.
21.2	Advertisements for betting tipsters must not be likely to be of particular appeal to under-18s.
21.3	Advertisements for betting tipster services must not make money-back guarantees.
21.4	Advertisements for betting tipster update-line services are acceptable only if the broadcaster is satisfied that the recorded messages are brief and the lines are a valid and necessary complement to the main-line service.
21.5	Before broadcasting an advertisement for a betting tipster service, a broadcaster must hold the tipster's name (not merely his or her business name) and his or her full, permanent business address.
21.6	Advertisements for a betting tipster service operating on a premium-rate phone line must include the service provider or information provider's usual trading name and contact details (see Section 22: Premium-rate Telephone Services).
21.7	Advertisements for betting tipsters who run, or are associated with, another betting tipster service must make that link clear.
21.8	Advertisements may include claims about a betting tipster's previous successful tips only if those claims are supported, before the relevant race, by proofing of all tips offered on his or her service on the day or during the period in question.
21.9	Advertisements for betting tipsters must not include claims about notional profits. Claims about previous profits must be proportionate and representative.
21.10	Advertisements for betting tipsters must not state or imply that success is guaranteed or that players could forge a long-term income by following the advertiser's tips.

21.11   Advertisements for betting tipsters may include claims about previous successful double, treble or other combination bets only if those claims are supported by proofing that the winners were clearly and specially tipped as a combination.

21.12   Profit, success or individual-win claims must not refer to odds.

21.13   If a change in circumstance would render it misleading, for example, if a race meeting were cancelled, an advertisement for a betting tipster must be not be repeated in its original form.

21.14   Advertisements for betting tipsters must not refer to a tip as a maximum bet or similar unless it is the only tip offered for that race. Claims about the success of a maximum tip are acceptable only if they are supported by advance proofing.

22

Premium-rate telephone services

Principle

The price and nature of premium-rate telephone services must be made clear. Advertisements that include premium-rate telephone numbers or short codes should comply with the PhonepayPlus Code of Practice.

Definition

Text short codes are premium-rate SMS services, which often consist of four or five digits and begin 5, 6 or 8.

Rules

22.1 Advertisements that include a premium-rate telephone number must comply with the PhonepayPlus Code of Practice.

22.2 Advertisements for premium-rate telephone services must include clear pricing information if the service generally costs 50 pence per call or more.

22.3 Advertisements for premium-rate children's services, services accessed by automated equipment or subscription services must always include clear pricing information.

22.4 Advertisements for premium-rate services must state the identity of the service provider or the information provider.

22.5 **Radio only –** If it is not included in the advertisement, radio broadcasters must retain and, on request, make available a non-premium-rate telephone number for the premium-rate service for customer care purposes. This rule does not apply if PhonepayPlus has expressly exempted a specific service or a number range from the need to provide a non-premium-rate telephone number for the premium-rate service.

22.6 **Television only –** Television advertisements for premium-rate services must include a non-premium-rate telephone number for customer care purposes. This rule does not apply if PhonepayPlus has expressly exempted a specific service or a number range from the need to provide a non-premium-rate telephone number for the premium-rate service.

22.7 Advertisements for services, excluding live or virtual-chat services, that normally involve a telephone call of at least five minutes must alert the audience that use of the service might involve a long call.

22.8   Advertisements for live premium-rate services must not appeal particularly to people under 18, unless those services have received prior permission from PhonepayPlus to target people under 18.

23

Telecommunications-based sexual entertainment services

Definition

Telecommunications-based sexual entertainment services are voice, text, image or video services of a sexual nature that are made available to consumers via a direct-response mechanism and are delivered over electronic communication networks.

'Encrypted elements of adult entertainment channels' are interpreted with reference to rule 1.24 of the Ofcom Broadcasting Code.

Rules

23.1 **Radio Central Copy Clearance –** Advertisements for telecommunications-based sexual entertainment services must be centrally cleared.

23.2 **Television only –** Advertising for telecommunications-based sexual entertainment services is only acceptable on:

    23.2.1 Encrypted elements of adult entertainment channels, or

    23.2.2 Channels that are licensed for the purpose of the promotion of the services and are appropriately positioned and labelled within an "Adult" or similar section of an Electronic Programme Guide.

23.3 **Television only –** Advertising for telecommunications-based sexual entertainment services must not be broadcast before 9pm or after 5:30am.

    On Digital Terrestrial Television, advertising for telecommunications-based sexual entertainment services must not be broadcast before 12am or after 5:30am.

24

Homeworking schemes

Principle

Homeworking scheme advertisements must neither mislead the audience nor exploit the susceptibilities or credulity of those seeking work.

Definition

Homeworking schemes are employment opportunities requiring participants to make articles, perform services or offer facilities at or from home. Participants can be self-employed or employed by a business.

Rules

24.1   Advertisements must not give a misleading impression of how homeworking schemes work or of the likely remuneration. Advertisements must make clear conditions, obligations or limitations that could reasonably be expected to influence a decision to participate in the scheme.

24.2   No homeworking scheme may be advertised:

24.2.1   if a charge or deposit is required to obtain information about the scheme

24.2.2   **Television only –** if it involves a charge for raw materials or components or

24.2.3   **Television only –** if the advertiser offers to buy goods made by the homeworker.

25

Instructional courses

Principle

Instructional course advertisements must neither mislead the audience nor exploit the susceptibilities or credulity of those seeking work.

Definition

Instructional courses are training or educational opportunities that typically offer instruction in a trade.

Rules

25.1   Advertisements offering a qualification, a course of instruction in a skill or a course that leads to a professional or technical examination must not exaggerate the resulting opportunities for work or remuneration.

25.2   Advertisements for a correspondence school or college may be broadcast only if the advertiser has given the broadcaster evidence of suitable and relevant credentials: for example, affiliation to a body that has systems for dealing with complaints and for taking disciplinary action; systems in place for regular review of members' skills and competencies and registration based on minimum standards for training and qualifications.

26

Services offering individual advice on consumer or personal problems

Rules

26.1   **Radio Central Copy Clearance –** Radio broadcasters must ensure that advertisements for services offering individual advice on consumer or personal problems are centrally cleared.

26.2   Services offering individual advice on consumer or personal problems may be advertised only if those advertisers have given the broadcaster evidence of suitable and relevant credentials: for example, affiliation to a body that has systems for dealing with complaints and for taking disciplinary action; systems in place for regular review of members' skills and competencies; registration based on minimum standards for training and qualifications; and suitable professional indemnity insurance covering the services provided.

26.3   **Television only –** Advertisements for commercial post-conception advice services offering individual advice on personal problems are not acceptable. (See Section 11, rule 11.11.)

27

Introduction and dating services

Background

Advertisements are acceptable, subject to rule 10.1.5: Prostitution and Sexual Massage and rule 10.2: Indirect Promotion. Broadcasters should take care to comply with Section 1: Compliance – in particular rule 1.2 on social responsibility and Section 4: Harm and Offence. Services operating through premium-rate telephone and text services are subject to Section 22: Premium-rate Telephone Services and the PhonepayPlus code.

For more information on the PhonepayPlus code go to: www.phonepayplus.org.uk

For information on the Data Protection Act 1998 go to: www.ico.gov.uk.

Rules

27.1   **Radio Central Copy Clearance –** Radio broadcasters must ensure advertisements for an introduction or dating agency are centrally cleared.

27.2   All claims relating to matching require substantiation.

27.3   Advertisements must not dwell excessively on loneliness or suggest that people without a partner are inadequate.

27.4   Broadcasters must satisfy themselves that advertisers give customers clear advice on precautions to take when meeting people through an advertisement for an introduction or dating agency.

27.5   Advertisements for an introduction or dating agency must not have particular appeal to people under 18. See Section 32: Scheduling.

28
Competitions

Rule

28.1   Competitions should be conducted fairly, prizes should be described accurately and rules should be clear and made known.

29

Private investigation agencies

Rules

29.1   **Radio Central Copy Clearance –** Radio advertisements for private investigation agencies must be centrally cleared.

29.2   Private investigation agencies may be advertised only if they have given the broadcaster evidence of suitable and relevant credentials: for example, affiliation to a body that has systems for dealing with complaints and for taking disciplinary action; registration based on minimum standards for training and qualifications, systems in place for regular review of members; skills and competencies and suitable professional indemnity insurance covering provided services.

30
Pornography

Definition

"Behind mandatory restricted access on adult entertainment channels" is interpreted with reference to rule 1.18 of the Ofcom Broadcasting Code.

"R-18 material" is classified as such by the British Board of Film Classification (BBFC): the BBFC's definition of the R-18 category appears on its website (www.bbfc.co.uk). The BBFC is responsible for classifying "video works", which are defined by, and subject to restriction under, the Video Recordings Act 1984.

Rules

30.1   **Radio Central Copy Clearance** – Advertisements for products coming within the recognised character of pornography may be broadcast only if they are centrally cleared.

30.2   Radio advertisements for R18-rated material are not permitted.

30.3   **Television only** – Advertisements for products coming within the recognised character of pornography are permitted behind mandatory restricted access on adult entertainment channels only.

30.3.1   **Television only** – Advertisements must not feature R18-rated material or its equivalent. That does not preclude advertisements for R18-rated material or its equivalent behind mandatory restricted access on adult entertainment channels.

30.3.2   **Television only** – Advertisements permitted under rules 30.2 and 30.2.1 must not feature material that comes within the recognised character of pornography before 10.00pm or after 5.30am.

30.3.3   Radio advertisements for R18-rated material are not permitted.

31

Other categories of radio advertisements that require central copy clearance

Rules

31.1   In addition to categories of radio advertisements specified in sections of this Code, these products and services require central copy clearance:

    31.1.1   adult shops

    31.1.2   stripograms

    31.1.3   escort agencies

    31.1.4   films, DVDs, videos, computer and console games that have an 18+ certificate or rating.

32
Scheduling

Principle

Broadcasters must take special care when scheduling advertisements that might be unsuitable for children or young persons or the audience of religious programmes or for broadcast around sensitive programming or news items.

Particular sensitivity is required for advertisements inserted in or around news or current affairs programmes in which a news item, especially one of a tragic nature, could completely transform the context in which an advertisement having an apparent connection with it could be perceived by viewers or listeners. A separation from news references might be inadequate and suspending the advertisement altogether to avoid distress or offence could be preferable.

Ofcom's television licensees must comply with the Ofcom Code on the Scheduling of Television Advertisements, which can be consulted on the Ofcom website, www.ofcom. org.uk.

Definitions

"Adjacent" refers to an advertising break immediately before or after the programme in question.

"Current" refers to a programme still running or scheduled to be resumed in the near future.

For the purposes of rule 32.12, a "politician" is defined as a Member of, or candidate for, the European or UK Parliament, other elected Assemblies in the UK or a local authority, a Member of the UK's House of Lords or a person prominent in a political party organisation.

"Children's programme" means a programme made for persons below the age of 16.

The restrictions given in rules 32.1 to 32.6 apply to sponsorship of the programme.

For broadcast television text and interactive television services, rule 32.20 sets out a list of products that must not be advertised around editorial content of particular appeal to children. For the avoidance of doubt, these rules apply to television text and interactive television services: 32.12, 32.13, 32.15 and 32.16.

Judging particular appeal of broadcast editorial content to children or young persons

Television

BCAP's Guidance Note "Audience indexing: identification of programmes likely to appeal to children and young people" sets out, in detail, how BCAP or the ASA would identify whether a programme has, or is likely to have, particular appeal to children or young persons.

Television Text and Interactive Television Services

When deciding whether an editorial page carried on broadcast television text or interactive television services has, or is likely to have particular appeal to children or young persons, BCAP or the ASA would consider, for example, the nature or subject of the editorial or the nature or subject of interactive prompts that have led or are likely to lead the child or young person directly to that page.

Radio

When deciding whether a station's programming has or is likely to have particular appeal to children or young persons, BCAP or the ASA would consider relevant factors, for example Radio Joint Audience Research (RAJAR) audience figures in the relevant time-slot, the nature of the station and programming and whether the advertisement was scheduled in the school run or in a time-slot when children are likely to be listening in large numbers.

Children

Advertisements that might frighten or distress children or are otherwise unsuitable for them (for example because they refer explicitly to sexual matters) must be subject to restrictions on times of transmission to minimise the risk that children in the relevant age group will see or hear them. That does not preclude well-considered daytime scheduling for such material but broadcasters should take account of factors, such as school holidays, that could affect child audience levels. Material that would be incomprehensible to pre-school children and could, therefore, reasonably be broadcast when they are viewing or listening with parents, might be more problematic in relation to older children.

For the avoidance of doubt, any given timing, programme category or age band restriction subsumes any other less severe restriction. Thus, on television, a 9.00pm restriction subsumes both a 7.30pm restriction as well as the restriction on scheduling in or adjacent to programmes commissioned for, principally directed at or likely to appeal particularly to children below the age of 16 or to programmes likely to have a significant child audience.

Special care needs to be exercised if a programme for, or likely to be of interest to, children is transmitted late in the evening or in the early hours of the morning, for example at Christmas. If such a programme is transmitted after 9.00pm, no advertisement carrying a timing restriction may be transmitted in or around that programme.

Children's Television Channels

Television channels devoted to children's programmes, or whose programmes are or are likely to be of particular appeal to children, will be unlikely to be able to carry at any time advertisements of the type restricted under rules 32.1 to 32.6. Thus, for instance, dedicated children's channels may not carry an advertisement for a product restricted under rule 32.2.2 or rule 32.5.1, namely: gambling and food or drink assessed as high in fat, salt or sugar (HFSS).

Rules

Scheduling of Television and Radio Advertisements

32.1   Broadcasters must exercise responsible judgement on the scheduling of advertisements and operate internal systems capable of identifying and avoiding unsuitable juxtapositions between advertising material and programmes, especially those that could distress or offend viewers or listeners.

Under-18s

32.2   These may not be advertised in or adjacent to programmes commissioned for, principally directed at or likely to appeal particularly to audiences below the age of 18:

32.2.1   alcoholic drinks containing 1.2% alcohol or more by volume (see rule 32.4.7)

32.2.2   gambling except lotteries, football pools, equal-chance gaming (under a prize gaming permit or at a licensed family entertainment centre), prize gaming (at a non-licensed family entertainment centre or at a travelling fair) or Category D gaming machines (see rule 32.4)

32.2.3   betting tipsters

32.2.4   slimming products, treatments or establishments (an exception is made for advertisements for calorie-reduced or energy-reduced foods and drinks, if they are not presented as part of a slimming regime and provided the advertisements do not use the theme of slimming or weight control)

32.2.5   religious matter subject to the rules on Religious Advertising in Section 15: Faith, Religion and Equivalent Systems of Belief

32.2.6   live premium-rate services, unless those services have received prior permission from PhonePay Plus to target people under 18.

Under-16s

32.3   Relevant timing restrictions must be applied to advertisements that, through their content, might harm or distress children of particular ages or that are otherwise unsuitable for them.

32.4   These products may not be advertised in or adjacent to programmes commissioned for, principally directed at or likely to appeal particularly to persons below the age of 16:

32.4.1   lotteries

32.4.2   football pools

32.4.3   equal-chance gaming (under a prize gaming permit or at a licensed family entertainment centre)

32.4.4   prize gaming (at a non-licensed family entertainment centre or at a travelling fair)

32.4.5   Category D gaming machines

32.4.6   medicines, vitamins or other dietary supplements

32.4.7   drinks containing less than 1.2% alcohol by volume when presented as low-alcohol or no-alcohol versions of an alcoholic drink

32.4.8   computer or console games carrying an 18+, 16+ or 15+ rating, including those that have not yet been classified, but which are expected by the publisher to secure a 15, 16+ or 18-rating.

Other Television Scheduling or Timing Restrictions: Children

Under-16s

32.5   These products may not be advertised in or adjacent to programmes commissioned for, principally directed at or likely to appeal particularly to audiences below the age of 16:

32.5.1   food or drink products that are assessed as high in fat, salt or sugar (HFSS) in accordance with the nutrient profiling scheme published by the Food Standards Agency (FSA) on 6 December 2005. Information on the FSA's nutrient profiling scheme is available on the FSA website at:

www.food.gov.uk/healthiereating/advertisingtochildren/nutlab/nutprofmod

32.5.2   matches

32.5.3   trailers for films or videos carrying an 18-certificate or 15-certificate (that does not preclude the scheduling in or adjacent to children's programmes of an advertisement containing brief extracts from such a film if those are used in connection with a promotional offer, derived from the film, for other types of product, subject to content).

Under-10s

32.6   These products may not be advertised in or adjacent to programmes commissioned for, principally directed at or likely to appeal particularly to children below the age of 10:

      32.6.1   sanitary protection products

      32.6.2   condoms.

Administering Medicines, Vitamins or Food Supplements to Children

32.7   Advertisements in which children are shown having a medicine, vitamin or other food supplement administered to them must not be broadcast before 9.00pm.

Children's Merchandise, Endorsements and Appearances by Persons from Children's Programmes

32.8   Advertisements for merchandise based on a children's programme must not be broadcast in the two hours before or after episodes or editions of that programme. The ASA and BCAP reserve the right to require a wider separation around some programmes, including a prohibition of any advertisement while a programme series is running.

32.9   Advertisements in which persons (including puppets) who appear regularly in any children's programme on any UK television channel present or endorse products of special interest to children must not be broadcast before 9.00pm.

32.10   To maintain a distinction between programmes and advertisements that is clear to a child audience, and to minimise any risk of confusion between the two, advertisements featuring a well-known personality or performer, or a person who takes a leading role in or whose appearance is central to a children's programme, must not be scheduled in breaks in or adjacent to that programme. For the purposes of this rule, cartoon and puppet characters are classed as "persons". For appearances by persons in chart programmes or programmes such as pop concerts, the restriction applies only to the breaks adjacent to the programme segment in which they appear. The rule does not apply to public service advertisements or to characters specially created for advertisements.

32.11   Advertisements containing appearances by persons in extracts from a children's programme must not be broadcast in the two hours before or after an episode or edition of the relevant programme.

Other Television Separations: Political

Scheduling of Television Advertisements that Feature Politicians

32.12   Once a General or European Election, a by-election for the UK, Scottish European Parliament or a local election (but not a local by-election) has been called, no advertisement featuring a UK politician may be shown in an area in which the election is to take place.

32.13   Advertisements featuring a candidate for a parliamentary by-election or a local authority election must not be shown in breaks in or adjacent to national news or election results programmes in the area where the election is to take place.

Exclusion of Certain Types of Television Advertisement in or Adjacent to Broadcasts of Parliamentary Proceedings

32.14   The following categories of advertisement may not be shown during live broadcasts of Parliamentary proceedings, or other programmes that include footage of Parliamentary proceedings other than brief news extracts:

32.14.1   advertisements that feature or refer to Members of Parliament, or Parliamentary parties, or with a Parliamentary setting

32.14.2   advertisements with direct and specific relevance to main items of Parliamentary coverage where these are known in advance.

For requirements applicable to advertisements in or adjacent to broadcasts of live Parliamentary proceedings, see Section 2: Recognition of Advertising.

Other Television Separations and Timing Restrictions

32.15   The ASA and BCAP reserve the right to issue directions requiring separation between certain advertisements or types of advertisement and certain programmes or types of programme for reasons or in ways that go beyond those already listed.

Those separations will usually be one of these:

32.15.1   not first or last in any advertisement break or both

32.15.2   not in the two hours before or after a certain programme

32.15.3   not for the duration of a programme series

32.15.4   neither for the duration of a programme series nor for a given period before and/or after the series

32.15.5   not before 7.30pm

32.15.6   not in or adjacent to programmes with a specific audience index.

32.16   On encrypted subscription services for which normal programme content-related scheduling constraints have been relaxed, advertisements appearing similarly encrypted on such a service may reflect the programme scheduling. For example, if the programme watershed has been moved on such a service, say, to 8.00pm, encrypted advertisements that attract a watershed timing restriction are permitted after 8.00pm, not only after 9.00pm. (See Section 1 of the Ofcom Broadcasting Code (Protection of the Under-Eighteens) www.ofcom.org.uk/tv/ifi/codes/bcode/.)

Scheduling of Radio Advertisements

32.17   Special care is required for these categories:

32.17.1   sensational newspapers, magazines or websites or their content

32.17.2   divination or the supernatural

32.17.3   sexual material, sex shops, stripograms or similar

32.17.4   sanitary protection products

32.17.5   family planning products (including contraceptives and pregnancy-testing products)

32.17.6   anti-drugs messages, including solvent abuse

32.17.7   HIV/AIDS prevention messages.

32.18   Violent or sexually explicit material must not be advertised in or adjacent to programmes targeted particularly at audiences below the age of 18.

Placement of Television Text and Interactive Advertisements

32.19   BCAP expects broadcasters to exercise responsible judgement in the placing of broadcast television text and interactive television advertisements and especially to consider the sensitivities of viewers likely to be exposed or attracted to particular editorial content.

Advertisements that are unsuitable for children (for example, because they might cause distress or because they refer explicitly to sexual matters) must be subject to restrictions on the time of transmission designed to minimise the risk that children in the relevant age group will see them.

32.20   Broadcast television text and interactive television advertisements for these product categories must not:

- be directly accessible from programmes commissioned for, principally directed at or likely to appeal particularly to children

- be directly accessible from advertisements that are adjacent to programmes commissioned for, principally directed at or likely to appeal particularly to children

- appear on editorial pages (text or interactive) that are likely to be of particular appeal to a significant audience of children

32.20.1   alcoholic drinks (including low-alcohol drinks)

32.20.2   films or DVDs carrying an 18-certificate or 15-certificate

32.20.3   medicines, vitamins or other dietary supplements

32.20.4   betting tips

32.20.5   computer or console games carrying an 18+, 16+ or 15+ rating

32.20.6   introduction and dating agencies

32.20.7   religious bodies. The only exception is advertising for publications, merchandise or other items if there is no recruitment or fund-raising link

32.20.8   advertisements that promote a product or service and invite consumers to buy that product or service via a direct response mechanism

32.20.9   matches

32.20.10   food or drink products that are assessed as high in fat, salt or sugar in accordance with the nutrient profiling scheme published by the Food Standards Agency (FSA). Information on the FSA's nutrient profiling scheme is available on the FSA website at:

www.food.gov.uk/healthiereating/advertisingtochildren/nutlab/nutprofmod

32.20.11   gambling, including lotteries.

Appendix 1:

Statutory framework for the regulation of broadcast advertising

Advertising Standards

1   The Communications Act 2003 requires Ofcom to set, and from time to time review and revise, codes containing such standards for the content of television and radio services licensed under the Broadcasting Acts 1990 and 1996 as seem to Ofcom to be best calculated to secure the standards objectives.

Sections 319(1), 319(3).

2   Ofcom has contracted-out its advertising standards codes function to the Broadcast Committee of Advertising Practice Limited (BCAP) under the Contracting Out (Functions Relating to Broadcast Advertising) and Specification of Relevant Functions Order 2004. That function is to be exercised in consultation with, and with the agreement of, Ofcom.

3   These provisions imposed on Ofcom by the Communications Act are therefore relevant to BCAP:

3.1   The standards objectives, insofar as they relate to advertising, include:

(a)   that persons under the age of 18 are protected;

(b)   that material likely to encourage or incite the commission of crime or lead to disorder is not included in television and radio services;

(e)   that the proper degree of responsibility is exercised with respect to the content of programmes which are religious programmes;

(f)   that generally accepted standards are applied to the contents of television and radio services so as to provide adequate protection for members of the public from inclusion in such services of offensive and harmful material;

(h)   that the inclusion of advertising which may be misleading, harmful or offensive in television and radio services is prevented;

(i)   that the international obligations of the United Kingdom with respect to advertising included in television and radio services are complied with [in particular in respect of television those obligations set out in Articles 3b, 3e, 10, 14, 15, 19, 20 and 22 of Directive 89/552/EEC (the Audi Visual Media Services Directive)];

(l)   that there is no use of techniques which exploit the possibility of conveying a message to viewers or listeners, or of otherwise influencing their minds, without their being aware, or fully aware, of what has occurred"

Section 319(2).

3.2   In setting or revising any such standards, Ofcom must have regard, in particular and to such extent as appears to them to be relevant to the securing of the standards objectives, to each of these matters:

"(a)   the degree of harm or offence likely to be caused by the inclusion of any particular sort of material in programmes generally, or in programmes of a particular description;

(b)   the likely size and composition of a potential audience for programmes included in television and radio services generally, or in television and radio services of a particular description;

(c)   the likely expectation of the audience as to the nature of a programme's content and the extent to which the nature of the programme's content can be brought to the attention of potential members of the audience;

(d)   the likelihood of persons who are unaware of the nature of the programme's content being unintentionally exposed, by their own actions, to that content;

(e)   the desirability of securing that the content of services identifies when there is a change affecting the nature of a service that is being watched or listened to and, in particular, a change that is relevant to the application of the standards set under this section...".

Section 319(4).

3.3   Ofcom must ensure that the standards from time to time in force under this section include:

"(a)   minimum standards applicable to all programmes included in television and radio services; and

(b)   such other standards applicable to particular descriptions of programmes, or of television and radio services, as appeared to them appropriate for securing the standards objectives."

Section 319(5).

3.4   Standards set to secure the standards objectives [specified in para 3(e) above] shall in particular contain provision designed to secure that religious programmes do not involve:

"(a)   any improper exploitation of any susceptibilities of the audience for such a programme; or

(b)   any abusive treatment of the religious views and beliefs of those belonging to a particular religion or religious denomination."

Section 319(6).

3.5   Standards set by Ofcom to secure the objectives [mentioned in 3(a), (h) and (i) above]:

"(a)   must include general provision governing standards and practice in advertising and in the sponsoring of programmes; and

(b)   may include provision prohibiting advertisements and forms of methods of advertising or sponsorship (whether generally or in particular circumstances)."

Section 321(1).

[NB: "Programme" includes an advertisement   Section 405(1)]

4   In addition the Broadcasting Act 1996 section 24(2) contains provisions permitting advertising on analogue ancillary services on channels 3, 4 and 5 only if directly related to advertising on the main service and digital ancillary services may carry no advertising of any kind.

5   BCAP works closely with the Committee of Advertising Practice to provide, insofar as is practicable and desirable, a co-ordinated and consistent approach to standards setting across broadcast and non-broadcast media.

6   The procedures for revision of the BCAP Codes, including consultation, are, to the extent applicable to BCAP's exercise of statutory functions, set out at section 324 of the Communications Act 2003.

7   Ofcom retains standards-setting functions for:

(a)   political advertising, the inclusion of which in television or radio services is prohibited by section 321(2) Communication Act, including decisions on whether an advertisement is "political advertising". But the rules on that remain in the BCAP Codes;

(b)   unsuitable programme sponsorship;

(c)   discrimination between advertisers who seek to have advertisements included in television and radio services. NB: Subject to that broadcasters, like publishers and other media, are entitled to refuse advertisements they do not want to carry;

(d)   the amount and scheduling of advertising, save for the scheduling of individual spot advertisements.

Investigation and complaints

8   The Communications Act requires Ofcom to establish procedures for the handling and resolution of complaints about the observance of standards (as set out in the BCAP Advertising Code) and to include conditions in licences for programme services requiring licence holders to comply with Ofcom's directions in relation to advertising standards.

Sections 325(2), (4) and (5).

9   The Medicines (Monitoring of Advertising) Regulations 1994 require Ofcom to consider complaints that an advertisement included, or proposed to be included, in a licensed service or S4C is an impermissible advertisement for a medicinal product, unless the complaint seems to Ofcom to be frivolous or vexatious.

10   Ofcom has contracted-out its powers of handling and resolving complaints about breaches of the BCAP Codes and the relevant provisions of The Medicines (Monitoring of Advertising) Regulations to the Advertising Standards Authority (Broadcast) Limited (ASA(B)) under The Contracting Out (Functions Relating to Broadcast Advertising) and Specification of Relevant Functions Order 2004.

11   ASA(B) will work closely with and under the umbrella of the Advertising Standards Authority to provide, insofar as is practicable and desirable, a co-ordinated and consistent approach to advertising standards regulation across broadcast and non-broadcast media.

12   Ofcom retains complaint investigation functions in respect of:

    (a)   political advertising;

    (b)   unsuitable sponsorship;

    (c)   discrimination between advertisers and

    (d)   scheduling of advertisements.

Statutory sanctions for breaches of advertising standards

13   Ofcom has similarly contracted-out its enforcement powers under the Communications Act, such that ASA(B) has these powers (including in relation to the Welsh Authority) for the purpose of securing compliance with the BCAP Codes, and with any additional requirements in licences for programme services in relation to advertising:

    (a)   to require a licence holder to exclude from its programme service an advertisement or to exclude it in certain circumstances (Section 325(5)(a));

    (b)   to require a licence holder to exclude from its service certain descriptions of advertisements and methods of advertising (whether generally or in certain circumstances) (Section 325(5)(b)). In respect of the additional licence requirements, such power may be exercised by ASAB only for impermissible medical advertisements;

    NB: Detailed reasons must be given for any of those actions in relation to a medicinal product advertisement and reference must be made to any remedy available in court and any time limit that must be met. (MMAR 1994 Regulation 9);

(c)   to require, from any person who to ASA(B) seems to be responsible for an advertisement, provision of evidence relating to the factual accuracy of any claim and to deem a factual claim inaccurate if such evidence is not so provided (Broadcasting Act 1990 s.4(1)(c) and 87(1)(d) and Broadcasting Act 1996 s.4(1)(c) and 43(1)(d)).

15   Ofcom retains these powers conferred by the Broadcasting Acts 1990 and 1996 and the Communications Act 2003:

(a)   to direct the broadcast of a correction or statement of findings

(b)   to impose a financial penalty or shorten a licence period and

(c)   to revoke a licence.

Overseas advertising

16   Licensees should seek BCAP's advice if they want to have any rules in the Code disapplied because the advertising is on a programme service addressed exclusively to audiences outside the UK.

17   An advertisement that is aimed specifically and with some frequency at audiences in the territory of a single party to the 1989 Council of Europe Convention on Transfrontier Television must, with some exceptions, comply with the television advertising rules of that party. This does not apply:

(a)   if the party is a Member State of the European Community or

(b)   if its television advertising rules discriminate between advertising broadcast on television services within its jurisdiction and that on services outside its jurisdiction or

(c)   if the UK Government has concluded a relevant bilateral or multilateral agreement with the party concerned.

Appendix 2:

Statutory framework for the regulation of broadcast advertising

1   Member States shall ensure that audiovisual commercial communications provided by media service providers under their jurisdiction comply with the following requirements:

(a)   audiovisual commercial communications shall be readily recognisable as such. Surreptitious audiovisual commercial communication shall be prohibited;

(b)   audiovisual commercial communications shall not use subliminal techniques;

(c)   audiovisual commercial communications shall not:

(i)   prejudice respect for human dignity;

(ii)   include or promote any discrimination based on sex, racial or ethnic origin, nationality, religion or belief, disability, age or sexual orientation;

(iii)   encourage behaviour prejudicial to health or safety;

(iv)   encourage behaviour grossly prejudicial to the protection of the environment.

(d)   all forms of audiovisual commercial communications for cigarettes and other tobacco products shall be prohibited;

(e)   audiovisual commercial communications for alcoholic beverages shall not be aimed specifically at minors and shall not encourage immoderate consumption of such beverages;

(f)   audiovisual commercial communication for medicinal products and medical treatment available only on prescription in the member State within whose jurisdiction the media service provider falls shall be prohibited;

(g)   audiovisual commercial communications shall not cause physical or moral detriment to minors. Therefore they shall not directly exhort minors to buy or hire a product or service by exploiting their inexperience or credulity, directly encourage them to persuade their parents or others to purchase the goods or services being advertised, exploit the special trust minors place in parents, teachers or other persons, or unreasonably show minors in dangerous situations.

Appendix 3:

The Consumer Protection from Unfair Trading Regulations 2008 (the CPRs) and the Business Protection from Misleading Marketing Regulations 2008 (the BPRs)

Background

As well as this Code, advertising is subject to legislation. See www.cap.org.uk for a non-exhaustive list.

The Consumer Protection from Unfair Trading Regulations 2008 (the CPRs)

One important piece of legislation that affects broadcast advertising is the Consumer Protection from Unfair Trading Regulations 2008 (CPRs). For the purpose of the Regulations and in this Appendix, "consumers" refers to individuals acting outside the course of their business. The CPRs prohibit unfair advertising to consumers, including misleading or aggressive advertising. Whenever it considers complaints that an advertisement misleads consumers or is unfair or aggressive to consumers, the ASA will have regard to the CPRs. That means it will take factors identified in the CPRs into account when it considers whether advertisements breach the BCAP Broadcast Advertising Code. Relevant principles established in the CPRs are summarised below. The summary is not an exhaustive statement of the effect of the Regulations and licensees who would like detailed guidance on the Regulations, as opposed to the Code, should seek legal advice.

Many rules in this Code prohibit misleading advertising. All rules that refer to misleading advertising should be read, in relation to business-to-consumer advertising, in conjunction with this summary:

Consumers

The likely effect of an advertisement is generally considered from the point of view of the average consumer who it reaches or to whom it is addressed. The average consumer is assumed to be reasonably well-informed, observant and circumspect.

In some circumstances, an advertisement may be considered from the point of view of the average member of a specific group:

- If the ad is directed to a particular group, the advertisement will be considered from the point of view of the average member of that group.
- If an advertisement is likely to affect the economic behaviour only of a identifiable group of people who are especially vulnerable, in a way that the advertiser could reasonably foresee, because of for example, mental or physical infirmity, age or credulity, the advertisement will be considered from the point of view of the average member of the affected group.

Misleading advertisements

Advertisements are misleading if they

- are likely to deceive consumers and
- are likely to cause consumers to take transactional decisions that they would not otherwise have taken.

"Transactional decisions" are consumers' decisions about whether to buy, pay for, exercise contractual rights in relation to, keep or dispose of goods or services. They include decisions to act and decisions not to act.

Advertisements can mislead consumers even if they do not include false information; for example, they can deceive through presentation or by omitting important information that consumers need to make an informed transactional decision.

Aggressive advertisements

Advertisements are aggressive if, taking all circumstances into account, they

- are likely to significantly impair the average consumer's freedom of choice through harassment, coercion or undue influence and
- are likely to cause consumers to take transactional decisions they would not otherwise have taken.

Unfair advertisements

Advertisements are unfair if they

- are contrary to the requirements of professional diligence and
- are likely to materially distort the economic behaviour of consumers in relation to the advertised goods or services.

The Business Protection from Misleading Marketing Regulations 2008 (the BPRs)

Business-to-business advertisements are subject to the Business Protection from Misleading Marketing Regulations 2008 (the BPRs). Under the BPRs, an advertisement is misleading if it:

- in any way, including its presentation, deceives or is likely to deceive the traders to whom it is addressed or whom it reaches and by reason of its deceptive nature, is likely to affect their economic behaviour
- or, for those reasons, injures or is likely to injure a competitor.

The BPRs also set out the conditions under which comparative advertisements, directed at either consumers or businesses, are permitted. This Code incorporates those conditions.

Index

INDEX

Note: All references are to paragraph numbers. Reference to the Appendices are indicated by the abbreviation "App", followed by Appendix number and paragraph number; for example, App 1: 2(b).

A

advertising recognition
    association with news bulletins 2.2
    association with other programmes 2.3
    distinguishable from editorial content 2.1
    distinguishable from programmes 2.4.1
    news and current affairs presenters (television) 2.4.2
    newsreaders (radio) 2.5
    parliamentary proceedings 2.4.3
advice services (consumer and personal)
    central clearance (radio) 26.1
    credentials 26.2
alcohol
    alcohol-masking products 10.1.1
    central clearance (radio) 19.1
    rules for alcohol advertisements
        Audiovisual Media Service Directive App 2: 1(e)
        children 19.15–19.16
        health and nutrition claims 19.18
        young adults 19.17
    rules for all advertisements
        content, strength and comparisons 19.10
        handling and serving 19.12
        illicit drugs 19.9
        immoderate consumption 19.11
        implying improved sexual activity 19.6
        implying solution to problems 19.7
        improved performance 19.8
        inappropriate behaviour 19.5
        irresponsible drinking 19.2
        machinery, driving and safety 19.13
        personal claims 19.3
        portrayal as taking priority 19.7
        social occasions 19.4
        sporting activities 19.13
        working environment 19.14
    scheduling 32.2.1, 32.4.7, 32.20.1
    treatments for alcohol and drug dependence 10.1.7, 11.21.2
animals in advertisements 4.11
Audiovisual Media Service Directive extracts App 2: 1

B

betting tipsters
    association with other betting tipster services 21.7
    central clearance (radio) 21.1

D

E

F

The BCAP Code: The UK Code of Broadcast Advertising

M

S

T

telecommunications-based sexual entertainment services
    central clearance (radio) 23.1
    Participation TV 3 (Ofcom) 23.2
television and television text-only advertisements
    faith, religion and other belief systems 15.4, 15.5, 15.7
    television text and interactive advertisements, scheduling 32.19–32.20
television-only advertisements
    advertising recognition 2.4
    children
        alcohol 19.15
        food and soft drinks 13.9–13.12
        price statements 5.12
    escort agencies 10.1.10
    harmful advertisements 4.6–4.7, 4.11
    health
        post-conception advice 11.11.2, 26.3
        teleshopping 11.12
    homeworking schemes 24.2.2–24.2.3
    pornography 30.3
    premium-rate telephone services 22.6
    privacy 6.1
    scheduling
        other separations 32.15–32.16
        political matters 32.12–32.14
    sexually explicit nature 22.9
    telecommunications-based sexual entertainment services 23.2
    see also television and television text-only advertisements
testimonials 3.45–3.48, 11.8, 12.14.3, 32.8–32.11
tobacco and tobacco-related products 10.1.3, App 2: 1(d)
    children 10.5
    non-tobacco products 10.4
    scheduling 32.5.2, 32.20.9
    smoking and use of tobacco products 10.3
trade marks and trade names 3.36, 3.42–3.44, 13.4
training courses *see* instructional courses

V

vitamins *see* food and soft drinks: supplements

W

weight control
    central clearance (radio) 12.1
    children 12.5
    energy-restricted diets 12.13
    establishments offering treatment 12.6.2, 12.11.1, 12.15
    health claims 12.8, 19.18
    inappropriate use of products 12.4